"A rare and special book that touches our inner selves with extraordinary courage, authenticity, and beauty. I have seen very few books with this kind of clarity and human depth. It will move you to tears and to joy. It will entertain and delight you, and it will make you a deeper and more compassionate human being."　　—John Robbins, author of *Diet for a New America*

"SPECTACULAR! I laughed and I cried . . . a tender and daring book that you'll never forget."
　　—Laura Davis, coauthor of *The Courage to Heal*

"I SEE MIRACLES IN MY LIFE EVERY DAY, AND ROTH IS ONE OF THE PEOPLE WHO HELPED MAKE THAT HAPPEN."　　—Anne Lamott in *Mademoiselle*

"*When Food Is Love* is Roth's seminal work. This is a big, beautiful, and important book. I cannot say enough about it. I hope everyone reads it."　　—Natalie Goldberg,
author of *Writing Down the Bones*

"She tells of her own experiences with a non-blink frankness cushioned by the gracefulness of her prose." —*Chicago Tribune*

"This book is A) good enough to eat, B) nourishing to the heart."
　　—Jack Kornfield, Buddhist teacher,
coauthor of *Seeking the Heart of Wisdom*

GENEEN ROTH, the founder of the Breaking Free® workshops, is a writer and teacher who has gained international prominence through her work with people who use food to cope with difficulties in their lives. She is the author of *Feeding the Hungry Heart, Breaking Free from Emotional Eating, Appetites,* and *Why Weight?* A frequent guest on television and radio programs, she has written for and been featured in *Time, Ms., New Woman, Family Circle,* and *Cosmopolitan.* She lives in California.

ALSO BY GENEEN ROTH

Feeding the Hungry Heart
Breaking Free from Emotional Eating
Why Weight?
Appetites

When Food Is Love

Exploring the Relationship
Between Eating and Intimacy

GENEEN ROTH

A PLUME BOOK

WORKSHOPS AND LECTURES

For a schedule of Geneen Roth's workshops and lectures, or if you are interested in bringing one to your area, please write her at the address below.

She welcomes any feedback or responses to *When Food Is Love*, but regrets that she is unable to answer individual letters.

Geneen Roth
P.O. Box 2852
Santa Cruz, CA 95063

PLUME
Published by the Penguin Group
Penguin Group (USA) Inc., 375 Hudson Street, New York, New York 10014, U.S.A.
Penguin Group (Canada), 90 Eglinton Avenue East, Suite 700, Toronto,
Ontario, Canada M4P 2Y3 (a division of Pearson Penguin Canada Inc.)
Penguin Books Ltd., 80 Strand, London WC2R 0RL, England
Penguin Ireland, 25 St. Stephen's Green, Dublin 2, Ireland (a division of Penguin Books Ltd.)
Penguin Group (Australia), 250 Camberwell Road, Camberwell, Victoria 3124, Australia
(a division of Pearson Australia Group Pty. Ltd.)
Penguin Books India Pvt. Ltd., 11 Community Centre, Panchsheel Park,
New Delhi – 110 017, India
Penguin Group (NZ), 67 Apollo Drive, Rosedale, North Shore 0632, New Zealand
(a division of Pearson New Zealand Ltd.)
Penguin Books (South Africa) (Pty.) Ltd., 24 Sturdee Avenue, Rosebank,
Johannesburg 2196, South Africa

Penguin Books Ltd., Registered Offices: 80 Strand, London WC2R 0RL, England

First published by Plume, a member of Penguin Group (USA) Inc. Previously published in a Dutton edition.

First Plume Printing, July 1992
40 39 38 37 36 35

LIBRARY OF CONGRESS CATALOGING-IN-PUBLICATION DATA
Roth, Geneen.
    When food is love : exploring the relationship between between eating and
intimacy / Geneen Roth.
        p.   cm.
    ISBN 978-0-452-26818-0
    1. Compulsive eating.   2. Intimacy (Psychology)   I. Title.
[RC552.C65R66   1992]
616.85'26—dc20   91–46198
                                                                     CIP

Printed in the United States of America
Original hardcover edition designed by Eve L. Kirch

To Matt
for singing to me about wishbones
in the middle of the night
and more

CONTENTS

Acknowledgments   ix

Introduction   1

Chapter 1. When Food Is Love   7

Chapter 2. Being In and Out of Control   27

Chapter 3. The Comfort of Suffering   53

Chapter 4. Wanting What Is Forbidden   75

Chapter 5. The One-Wrong-Move Syndrome   95

Chapter 6. Grieving for the Lost Years   113

Chapter 7. Being a Victim, Being Powerful   135

Chapter 8. Being Strong in the Broken Places   163

Chapter 9. When Love Is Love   185

ACKNOWLEDGMENTS

I am grateful to have friends who are willing to take the time to understand, question, and deepen my writing. For welcoming each chapter as I finished it and for gluing me to life, I thank Sara Friedlander. For her superb, insightful, and challenging reading of the manuscript, I thank Laura Davis. For offering her brilliance, her impeccable line editing, and the perspective of half a lifetime of friendship, I thank Jace Schinderman. For providing a novelist's perspective and a letter I will treasure always, I thank Eddie Lewis. For questioning and pushing me to rewrite more than a few chapters, I thank Cliff Friedlander. For supporting what I hoped was true, I thank Katy Hutchins. For the glorious pleasure of writing together and for seeing my writer's soul, I thank Natalie Goldberg.

I would also like to thank:

Maggie Phillips, for teaching me about the content of the book by encouraging me to speak the unspeakable and by being a model of love that endures; Sil Reynolds, for giving herself to me as workshop assistant, teaching associate, and sister; Ruth Wiggs, my mother, for teaching me about courage, fortitude, and healing by flying to California to read the book with me; Karen Russell, for her willingness to share her joy and her sorrow, and for the example she sets of a life lived with passion and grace; Maureen Nemeth, for her efficiency in running the Breaking Free office and for the freedom to write it gives me; Nancy Wechsler, for her reassuring, wise counsel; Michaela Hamilton, Elaine Koster, Alexia Dorszynski, and the sales force at Dutton, for their confidence in me and their commitment to my work; Angela Miller, for persevering despite and because of everything we've been through together; the woman at the 1988 Omega workshop, for suggesting the title of this book; the participants in my workshops, for touching and inspiring me with their longing and their love; Jack Kornfield, Joseph Goldstein, Stephen Levine, and Emmanuel, for blessing me with teachings that open my heart and remind me where home is.

Peg Parkinson—my first editor, my friend, and my mentor—died after editing the manuscript and before its publication. Her spirit is woven throughout the book and inside me.

LATE FRAGMENT

And did you get what
you wanted from this life, even so?
I did.
And what did you want?
To call myself beloved, to feel myself
beloved on the earth.

—Raymond Carver

When
Food Is
Love

INTRODUCTION

When I was eleven, I began dieting, and for the next seventeen years I spent the largest part of every day thinking about what I wanted to eat that I shouldn't and what I should eat that I didn't want. As I began spinning a world in which there were only two players, food and me, my capacity to be affected by other people diminished greatly. By the time I was twenty-eight, nothing mattered to me except being thin.

After the publication of *Feeding the Hungry Heart* and *Breaking Free*, after I reached my natural weight and stayed there, I discovered that it wasn't *being* thin I wanted, it was *getting* thin.

As long as my attention was consumed by what I ate, what size clothes I wore, how much cellulite I had on the backs of my legs, and what my life would be like when I finally lost the weight, I could not be deeply hurt by another person. My obsession with weight was more dramatic and certainly more immediate than anything that happened between me and a friend or lover. When I did feel rejected by someone, I reasoned that she or he was rejecting my body, not me, and that when I got thin, things would be different.

I thought I wanted to be thin; I discovered that what I wanted was to be invulnerable.

Then I met Matt, a man with whom I wanted to spend my life. After the initial bliss of falling in love, I came face to face with myself and discovered I was like a child who spends her time in a fantasy world and doesn't know how to play with real children. I didn't know how to engage myself deeply with a person, only with food.

I had friends, good friends, a best friend. I had lovers; I had been in one relationship for seven years. But I am not speaking of friends or lovers. I am speaking of intimacy, of surrender, trust, and a willingness to face, rather than run from, the worst of myself.

The wonderful thing about food is that it doesn't leave, talk back, or have a mind of its own. The difficult thing about people is that they do. Food was my lover for seventeen years and demanded nothing of me. Which was exactly the way I wanted it.

A few years ago, *Glamour* magazine conducted a survey of 33,000 women called "Feeling Fat in a Thin Society." Seventy-five percent of the respondents said they felt too fat. The women were asked if their weight affected their feelings about themselves; 96 percent said it did. Given the choice of losing weight, happiness in a relationship, success at work, or hearing from an old friend, nearly half the women said losing weight would make them happier than anything else.

The issue is the same and different for men. Most men are less focused on their weight than women are, but there are many men for whom judgments about their weight and low self-confidence are painfully connected. These men have a different burden from that of women, because it is rarely acceptable for them to express or receive support when they are in this kind of pain—especially since it's about a 'woman's issue.' For both men and women, the focus on food provides a distraction from underlying issues of trust and intimacy. We'd rather lose weight than be close to another human being. We'd rather focus on our bodies than love or be loved. It's safer: we know where the pain will come from, we're in control.

During the first two years I spent with Matt, I found myself struggling with the same patterns I thought I had resolved years before with my eating. Worse, I felt like a child again, reacting to the long-forgotten fears of being left, being unloved, being crazy. As I struggled on a daily basis to bring myself to the present moment and remind myself that I was thirty-five, not five, and this was Matt, not my mother or father, I was struck by the similarities between eating and loving.

Eating is a metaphor for the way we live; it is also a metaphor for the way we love. Excessive fantasizing, creating drama, the need to be in control, and wanting what is forbidden are behaviors that block us from finding joy in food or relationships. And some of the same guidelines that enable us to break free from compulsive behavior—learning to stay in the present, beginning to value ourselves now, giving the hungry child within us a voice, trusting our physical and emotional hungers, and teaching ourselves to receive pleasure—enable us to be intimate with another person.

For the past twelve years I've been leading workshops about breaking free from compulsive eating, and recently, about eating and intimacy. I work with a few thousand people each year. Two out of four women in my workshops have been sexually abused as children; more than half of the participants are adult children of alcoholics. Most people come from troubled families. Yet they believe that food and weight are their biggest problems. They believe that if they lost weight, they would be fine, although most of them have lost significant amounts of weight five, ten, twenty times in their lives—and weren't fine. They regained the weight and then went on another diet.

Americans spend $33 billion a year on losing weight. Twenty million women have eating disorders. Twenty-five percent of all men are constantly dieting, 50 percent of all women. And nine out of ten people who lose weight on a diet gain it back. For those who fail on a diet this year, there will be 30,000 new diet plans next year to choose from.

Diets don't work because food and weight are the symptoms, not the problems. The focus on weight provides a convenient and culturally reinforced distraction from the reasons why so many people use food when they are not hungry. These reasons are more complex than—and will never be solved with—willpower, counting calories, and exercise. They have to do with neglect, lack of trust, lack of love, sexual abuse, physical abuse, unexpressed rage, grief, being the object of discrimination, protection from getting hurt again. People abuse themselves with food because they don't know they deserve better. People abuse themselves because they've been abused. They become self-loathing, unhappy adults not because they've experienced trauma but because they've repressed it.

When Food Is Love speaks to the heart of why people turn to food. It explores the messages we received as children, how we translate them into messages of self-hate, and how we pass this pain on to other people, including our children. And it explores the importance of taking responsibility for change in the present rather than feeling victimized by the pain of the past. Because our patterns of eating were *formed* by early patterns of loving, it is necessary to understand and work with both food and love to feel satisfied with our relationship to either.

This is a personal book. I grew up with a physically abusive mother who was addicted to drugs and alcohol; my father was often absent or emotionally unavailable. The book is about the past and how it affected the way I ate and loved; it is about the present and learning to be intimate with Matt, after living in a self-absorbed world of compulsion for so long. It is about speaking the unspeakable, healing, and moving on, and it is about the celebration of being whole.

It is also about many of the people with whom I've worked and from whom I've received letters. With their permission, I tell their stories, their struggles, their victories.

When Food Is Love is a book about intimacy as seen through the filter of compulsion. And it is a book about the fears and the joys of taking that filter away. It is not a typical self-help book in the sense that it does not list specific exercises and guidelines to practice on a daily basis. The information is revealed in the storytelling. It is a book that I hope will inspire you to remember and acknowledge the pieces of your life you've minimized or shut away or forgotten. These pieces deeply affect the way you eat and love, and keep you from living with creativity and passion, self-respect and a belief in your own effectiveness.

In my previous books, I wrote about the process of resolving compulsive behavior—specifically, compulsive eating. But curing compulsive behavior is not enough. The next step is to engage deeply with ourselves and with other people. To open our hearts and let love in. This book is about taking that step.

CHAPTER

1

When Food
Is Love

I fell in love for the first time when I was in sixth grade. His name was Martin Levy and he was a senior in high school. Martin had thick ropy muscles, agate eyes, and a face that reflected the brawny days of summer. On Carnival Day, I asked him to marry me; he said yes. We walked into the marriage booth, which was decorated in red and white crepe paper streamers, and the social studies teacher, Mr. Ogden, pronounced us husband and wife. Martin squeezed my hand, I blushed, and then he kissed me. On The Lips. I framed our marriage certificate and hung it next to my bed so it could be part of my dreams. I played "Born Too Late," a song by the Pony Tails, over and over and over again until my brother smashed it in half because he couldn't stand to hear it one more time.

I started dieting the same year I met Martin. At first, I believed that if I were thin, I would be beautiful—and that if I were beautiful, Martin would take me seriously. After he graduated, I just wanted to be beautiful. And for the next seventeen years, my main passion in life was not a relationship but my weight. Many other dramas were playing themselves out before me: my parents were desperately unhappy, my first real boyfriend died of cancer, my friend Candy's mother killed herself, my brother was going to school, stoned, in a top *h*at and tails, but through it all, I built a cool blue shelter in a corner of my body that promised a life of tenderness and beauty . . . if I could just get thin.

Then I got thin. Thirteen years ago, I stopped dieting and lost forty pounds. I wrote a book about it. I talked on television about it. I wrote another book about it. I waited for tenderness and beauty to sift through my cool blue shelter.

And then I realized that beneath my longing to be thin was the belief that being thin would mean being in love. When I pictured myself thin, I never saw myself alone. Being thin meant being happy and being happy meant not being alone. Being thin meant being in love. Suddenly, I wanted a partner as much as I had wanted to be thin.

But it was not politically correct to put one's life on hold and wait for the perfect partner, so I went about creating the kind of life I wanted without one. I moved to my dream house, a small beach cottage with skylights and glass doors and plum trees. I started workshops, and with the success of the books, slowly built my own business. Life was good. I had friends whom I loved. I had work that was a true expression of my values. I was thin and healthy. But I was waiting.

I told myself that if I spent the rest of my life without a partner, I would still be living fully. Think of Katharine Hepburn, I told myself. She is vibrant and creative and living alone. *Everyone* ends up alone, I reasoned. It's better to be alone than to be lonely with someone I don't love. I believed it all. But I was still dreaming of moony kisses and entwined bodies.

In many ways, I was still the fifteen-year-old whispering in a darkened room to my friend Jil about falling in love and the passion that accompanies it.

"Do you think it hurts when he puts it inside of you?" Jil had asked then.

"I don't think so," I said. "Otherwise why would so many

people be making such a big deal over sex? I mean, if it hurts, what's the point?"

"What do you think it *feels* like?" she asked, her voice beginning to rise.

"I don't know."

Jil sat up and turned on the light. She was too excited to sleep. I rolled on my side to face her. The lace on the collar of her Lanz nightgown was caught under the yoke. An oversized Raggedy Ann doll surrounded by a menagerie of stuffed animals was perched on the ottoman.

"I think it must be the most wonderful feeling in the world," Jil said. "You look into his eyes, he looks into your eyes, and you both moan. For a moment, the two of you are one person. Can you imagine anything better?"

"No," I murmured, "I can't."

I fell asleep dreaming of a man with curly hair and nickel-round eyes.

Nineteen years later, I was still dreaming about him.

In the afternoons, when the sun was lighting the stars on the quilt, I would imagine his sitting on the bed, watching me. I would act as if he already loved the speck of gold in my right eye, the way I said hello when I answered the phone, the shape of my face, the texture of my skin. And I would feel hopeful, complete.

In the evenings, when the empty bowl of the night sky erased the day, I would turn on the light and go to the mirror. "This face is clear and bright," I would say aloud. "If I were a man and saw you, I would want to know you. If I were a man, I could love you."

After my book *Breaking Free* was published, my friend Babs told me that I had to make more of an effort. She said, "How do you expect to meet a man when you work with women, write for women, and spend all your time with women friends? Go out more. Go dancing. Go to parties."

My best friend, Sara, said, "Do you expect him to ring your doorbell and come walking into your house? You need to do more things. Don't be solitary."

Ellen said, "One is all it takes. You'll find him. Just don't worry so much."

I was afraid that I was not enough of whatever it took—and too much of what it didn't take—to be in a committed relationship.

Babs urged me to put a personal ad in the local paper. She said, "It's the new way to meet men; it's better than going to bars or parties or evening classes. And this way you can be very specific about what you want."

When she moved in with the man she met through *her* ad, I decided she was right.

I spent the next four months writing my own ad. I couldn't decide whether I should describe myself as "attractive" or "very attractive," whether I should mention that I didn't like Woody Allen movies or that I liked chocolate. I didn't want to say that I had written books about eating because I didn't want anyone to recognize me, but I didn't want to be dishonest either. After I revised the ad a few hundred times, I bribed Maureen, my office manager, to bring it to the newspaper so that they would think she was placing it. The final wording was:

A lover who is a friend. I am a vibrant, attractive 34-year-old Jewish SWF with fulfilling and successful work, a frequent sense of humor, and a desire to be in a relationship with a man who will be a friend as well as a lover. At different times, I am some or all of these things: playful, serious, outrageous, tender, and perceptive. I like being outside, being healthy, dancing, chocolate, noticing the extraordinary in the ordinary. Woody Allen movies depress me. I am looking for a single professional man, 30–45 years old, who is kind, comfortable and honest with himself (a *mensch*), who knows how to laugh, take good care of himself, listen, not leave when it gets hard, and who believes that his life will be enhanced by growing in a relationship with a woman. I wouldn't turn down a gourmet cook.

I got seventy replies, ten photographs, two bouquets of roses, three poems, and a loaf of onion bread. My friend Ellen and I divided the letters into three piles: yes, no, and maybe. Sara and I reread the yeses and set up a schedule whereby I was supposed to call two or three men a night. I didn't want to do it. I didn't want to suffer the embarrassment of the first few minutes of talking to men I didn't know and probably wouldn't like. I wanted to forget the whole thing, throw the letters away, become a Jewish priestess. Instead, Sara and I made a deal: I would dial the phone number from my office, and as soon as the ringing started, she would pick up the extension in the adjoining room so that we could see each other and signal important messages back and forth.

"Hello?"

"Hi. My name's Geneen. I'm calling because, um, because I put an ad in the paper and you answered it."

"Which ad was that? I answered quite a few."

At this point, I would give Sara an "Oh-my-God-how-did-I-get-myself-into-this?" look and she would give me a "Will-you-shut-up-and-answer-him?" stare.

I met computer programmers, psychologists, construction workers. I met a man who bit a burglar's ear off in a fight, a man who lived with his mother and his ex-wife, and a man who owned fifteen cats, three finches, and a goldfish. Each time I talked to someone I liked, I'd construct a visual image of him to match his voice. I was always wrong. One man told me he was tall and lanky; when I met him, he was 5'4" and very round. Another man told me he was "very handsome" and that I wouldn't be disappointed. He didn't tell me that his front tooth was missing or that he had a rose tattoo on his right cheek. After five weeks of meeting strangers on the steps of the post office or next to the pumpernickel raisin bread in Gayle's Bakery, I hadn't met anyone I wanted to see again.

Then I met Matt. Not through my ad.

I heard him speak at a conference at which we were both presenters and I was enchanted. He was compelling, funny, and sexy. I wanted to meet him. When I saw him the next day, I introduced myself. I told him I thought his talk was wonderful and that I had the same sunglasses as he was wearing. He said thank you and that I had good taste in sunglasses. He kept walking.

On the last day of the conference, psychologist Virginia Satir was giving the closing speech in an auditorium filled with a thousand participants. I was sitting in the center of the room in the center of a row. From the corner of my eye, I noticed Matt walking toward the door. Without thinking, I excused myself, wove past knees and legs, tripped over a purse, and made my way to the back of the room. When we were face to face, I said, "I introduced myself to you yesterday but I don't think you noticed me. My name is Geneen Roth and I wanted to tell you again how moved I was by your talk."

This time, he noticed me.

❧✖❧

After our first date, I was wild with excitement. Crazed by the edge of passion and possibilities. I liked the way he looked at me, the way he talked about his work, the way he was interested in mine. I liked the space between his front teeth, the line of his nose, the lilt of his laugh. When he left a message on my answering machine that said, "I just want you to know how glad I am that I met you and that you are in my life," I told Sara that I must be dreaming. "A man who says what he feels. I can't believe it."

On our second date, we went to the botanical gardens. Sitting next to the row of bearded purple irises he said, "I know it's insanely early to tell you that I want to see only you, but I want to see only you. I think I'm falling in love with you."

I wanted to drink the flowers, eat the colors, cover his face with lavender kisses. "Don't wake me up," I said to him. "If this is a dream, don't wake me up."

For eight months, I woke up singing. I smiled so much my mouth hurt. I kissed him so much my lips got numb. I liked myself better when I was with him; I was kinder, calmer, happier. I was pulsing with love, blooming with light.

And then slowly, I came back to myself.

Someone once came to a workshop after she had lost seventy-five pounds on a diet. She stood up in front of 150 people and, with her voice shaking, said, "I feel like I've been robbed. My best dream has been taken away. I really thought that losing weight was going to change my life. But it only changed the outside of me. The inside is still the same. My mother is still dead and my father still beat me when I was growing up. I'm still angry and lonely and now I don't have getting thin to look forward to."

After waiting all our lives for tenderness and beauty to arrive in the form of being thin or being in love, it can be devastating to discover that neither one can be found in either one. Not when the expectation is that we will lose ourselves. Or find ourselves.

❧✖❧

Compulsion is despair on the emotional level. The substances, people, or activities that we become compulsive about are those that we believe capable of taking our despair away.

Despair.

I felt it first as a child. I didn't have a name for it then. It was the feeling I carried inside my body that my world was about to rip apart and there was nothing I could do about it. No one I could talk to about it. No way of preventing it, no way of making anything better.

I look at my life now. There is nothing to despair about. But sometimes, often, something will happen, and everything around me—the sky, my body, Matt's face—will turn to clay.

❀✖❀

It is nine months after my first date with Matt. We are at La Guardia airport; it is afternoon. Our plane has just landed from Bermuda, where Matt and I have spent five days reading novels, making love, eating papaya for lunch, and filling the vases in our room with crimson red bougainvillea. We are walking to the taxi stand, where he is going to get a cab into New York City and I am going to get a bus to Rhinebeck. I am dreading the separation, not because I am lonely when I am alone (I thrive on solitude); not because I have nothing to do for the next five days (I am going to Rhinebeck to lead a workshop). I am dreading the separation because it strikes a familiar terror in me. I don't want him to leave.

(*If you leave, I will have nothing left*. We were living in the brown apartment: brown chairs, brown carpet, brown couch. I was three years old. She was getting ready to walk out the door. I started to scream. *If you leave me, Mama, nothing will be left of me*. I was crouched in a corner of the room wearing my corduroy blue pants and red tie shoes. When she walked out the door, I lay down on the brown floor and sobbed. Ann, our babysitter, appeared. She picked me up and put me on the end of the vacuum cleaner and gave me rides all afternoon. When my mom returned, she gave me a red, white, and blue scarf.)

(*If you leave, I will have nothing left*. We were living in the black-and-white house. Black-and-white chairs, black-and-white marble floor, black-and-white couch. I was eleven. She was lying in bed in the afternoon. She was telling me that she wanted a divorce. I began to cry. *What will happen to me?* I asked. *Who will I live with? Where will I go? Don't leave, Mom. If you do, I will have nothing left.*)

Matt and I have arrived at the taxi stand and he turns to say goodbye, bends his face to mine to kiss me. The panic is trapped in my throat, a blackbird thrashing to get loose.

I can't make the jump to tomorrow. I can't see myself walking, talking, working without him. Everything stops here. *If he leaves, I will have nothing left.*

He says, "I will call you at your mom's house on Sunday night."

I say, "Someday I'm going to go on a trip and you won't be able to reach me and you will miss me terribly." He looks startled.

He says, "That is what is happening now—you won't be reachable by phone until Sunday and I am going to miss you."

I say nothing. I want him to say, "I'll cancel my meetings and come with you to Rhinebeck." I want him to say, "I can't stand these separations—let's never be apart again." I want him to say, "I love you too much to leave." Instead, he says, "I love you, Geneen. I know this is hard for you; you forget that we are going to have many more days together, years together. Leaving is not the end. I have to go now. I have a meeting in half an hour. Do you want to say anything?" I shake my head no. He looks at me intently for a moment, kisses me lightly, turns to get in a cab.

I hate him.

Loving him was supposed to take the pain away. Instead, it brings it up: The years of coming home from school and wandering from empty room to empty room. I would sit on the beige-velvet couch and stare at the still-life painting of a wheel of cheese, an apple, a knife with a black handle. I would go into the kitchen and open the refrigerator door, close it, and then open it. Close it. Open it. Eat. I would walk into my mother's bedroom and smell the traces of Joy perfume, open her jewelry drawer, pick up a pair of gold hoop earrings and hold them to my ears. I would smile at myself in the mirror, pretend that I was at a party, say hello and raise my eyebrows.

I wanted my mother. I wanted my father to come home for dinner and tell my mother that she was pretty and that he loved her. I wanted my mother to come home for dinner and tell me that I was pretty and that she loved me. I wanted her to tell me that our world was not going to fly apart at any moment and that I could stop trying so hard to be good.

Loving Matt was supposed to take the pain away. All of it. From all the years. I thought that having someone to sleep with and talk with and eat with was going to take the pain away. But there are many moments—my moment at the airport is one of them—when I feel as if I am wandering from the living room to the kitchen to my mother's bedroom and that there is no one home.

❧✖❧

Compulsion is despair on the emotional level. Compulsion is the feeling that there is no one home. We become compulsive to put someone home.

All we ever wanted was love.

We didn't *want* to become compulsive about anything. We did it to survive. We did it to keep from going crazy. Good for us.

Food was our love; eating was our way of *being* loved. Food was available when our parents weren't. Food didn't get up and walk away when our fathers did. Food didn't hurt us. Food didn't say no. Food didn't hit. Food didn't get drunk. Food was always there. Food tasted good. Food was warm when we were cold and cold when we were hot. Food became the closest thing we knew of love.

But it is only a substitute for love. Food is not, nor was it ever, love.

Many of us have been using food to replace love for so many years that we no longer know the difference between turning to food for love and turning to love for love. We wouldn't recognize love if it knocked us over.

Not because we are ignorant but because if we've never been loved well, we don't know what love feels like, what love *is* like. And it follows that if we have not been loved well, we cannot love ourselves well. Compulsive behavior, at its most fundamental, is a lack of self-love; it is an expression of a belief that we are not good enough.

☺✖☺

A writer friend came to visit yesterday. She brought me fresh-picked blackberries in a white porcelain bowl. Sitting at the kitchen table, Lyn propped her head on her hand and told me that she was scheduled to attend a conference the following weekend and didn't want to go. I asked her why. She said, "Because I'll see Kristin and I've gained ten pounds since the last time I saw her." Before I could say anything, she corrected herself: "Actually, I've only gained six."

She continued, "You know, Kristin and I used to weigh exactly the same. I used to have a body just like hers."

"Why would you want to have a body like Kristin's?" I asked, remembering that Kristin had bony hips and feet that splayed out.

"Doesn't everyone?" she asked.

I shook my head no. I asked her what she would be spending her time thinking about if it weren't her body. She said, "I'd be worrying that I am a terrible writer."

Later, alone at the table, I was thinking about Lyn's visit. I was thinking that compulsions are rarely what they seem to be. I was thinking that concerns about our bodies cover deeper concerns about other things that cover even more basic concerns about ourselves. Being a terrible writer, I thought, is not what Lyn is afraid of.

When I spoke to her the next day, she said, "You know, I realized yesterday when I got home that I didn't tell you what the bottom line was. You asked what I would be worrying about and I said my writing but that isn't it."

"What is?"

She took a deep breath. So did I.

"I know this is going to sound corny, but I think what I am afraid of is not being good enough. That something deep down is wrong with me and that I am not worth loving."

※✕※

Food and love. We begin eating compulsively because of reasons that have to do with the kind and amount of love that is in our lives or that is missing from our lives. If we haven't been loved well, recognized, understood, we arrange ourselves to fit the shape of our situations. We lower our expectations. We stop asking for what we need. We stop showing the places that hurt or need comfort. We stop expecting to be met. And we begin to rely on ourselves and only ourselves to provide sustenance, comfort, and pleasure. We begin to eat. And eat.

※✕※

Trina was three years old when her mother left her at her grand-mother's house, saying she would come back for her the next day. The next day, Trina sat on the front porch of her grand-mother's farmhouse and waited. She waited the next day. And the next. Every day for eight years, Trina waited for her mother to come back. And every day for eight years, her grandmother complained about having to take care of Trina. More than com-plained. She beat Trina. With a switch and until she bled. Every day for eight years. When Trina would go to school bruised and swollen, the teachers would ask her what happened. They'd say,

"Trina! Has someone been hitting you?" And she'd say, "No, ma'am. I fell down the stairs" or "I tripped when I was running to school this morning" or "I knocked into the refrigerator." She was afraid that if she got her grandmother in trouble, she would get beaten even harder. Or worse, that they'd do something to her grandmother and then she would have nowhere to go.

Trina survived. Some children would have survived by turning to drugs. Some would have run away. Some children would have become alcoholic. Or ended up in a mental institution. Trina did something else, two things really. The first was that she kept a rubber band around her wrist, and after each time her grandmother hit her, she'd use it to snap herself back into the present moment. She became very good at leaving her body. "When I was getting a beating," Trina says, "I'd think of a lesson we had learned that day at school—how to spell 'princess' or something. I'd think of flowers in the yard, the camellias when they first open, the yellow specks on the inside. When my grandmother finished beating me, she'd go back into the house and I'd stay outside and pop the rubber band on my wrist. I knew it was going to hurt a little, but the sound of it popping and the tingles of it on my wrist would make me come back from thinking about red flowers to where I was right then: in front of my grandmother's house with chores to do that I'd better start doing so that she didn't come out and hit me again."

The second thing Trina did was sneak food from the kitchen and store it under her bed. Boxes and cans and bags of food. "My grandmother kept sweets in the dresser in her bedroom," she said, "underneath the bras with the wires in them. And whenever she watched TV, I would sneak into her room, put some of the candies under my shirt, and hide them between the mattress and box spring of my bed. Sometimes," she said, "I would take cans of food from the kitchen and put them under there, too. In the middle of the night, when my grandmother was sleeping, I would turn on my night light, get out my can opener, and eat. Eating, especially food that I had taken from my grandmother's drawer, made me feel like I was someone special."

If Trina could not get her grandmother's love, she would steal her food.

The messages she received about herself and the world around her were:

> I did something wrong and that's why my mom isn't coming back. I am bad.
>
> People lie. It's better not to believe them.
>
> Loving hurts.
>
> When someone leaves me, they never come back.
>
> I need too much, want too much. That's why my grandmother doesn't like having me here.
>
> If I could do everything my grandmother tells me to do, I would be good and then my mom would come back.
>
> My grandmother is a grown-up; she knows best and she hits me every day. If I were good on the inside, I wouldn't get hit on the outside.
>
> It's better to eat than to care about someone because food doesn't leave and moms do. Food doesn't hit and grandmothers do.

When Trina was eleven, her mother returned. I met her when she was thirty-three. In twenty-nine years, she has gained and lost over 1500 pounds. In the past ten years, she has been married, divorced, a mother, and remarried. About her present marriage she says, "I cannot let my husband in. If he goes away on a business trip for two days, I feel like I have to start all over again with him when he returns; it is as if he is a stranger, constantly a stranger."

She spent too many years waiting for her mother to return; she will not feel the pain of waiting again. During his time away, she eats to assuage the loneliness. She focuses on how fat she is and how much weight she should lose and the clothes she will buy when she is thin. She transfers the pain of waiting to the pain of being fat. When her husband returns, they must cover a distance of eight years of confusion, loneliness, and betrayal to be intimate again. Or at all.

For it is not just when her husband leaves that she closes herself to him; Trina's experience of love is that it hurts. Love hurts. People lie. People leave. When her husband leaves on a trip, she is not surprised. She knows that people betray you, and she has carefully protected herself from feeling the pain of his (or anyone's) betrayal: She has taken another lover, one who will never leave: Food.

☺✖☺

Love and compulsion cannot coexist.

Love is the willingness and ability to be affected by another human being and to allow that effect to make a difference in what you do, say, become.

Compulsion is the act of wrapping ourselves around an activity, a substance, or a person to survive, to tolerate and numb our experience of the moment.

Love is a state of connectedness, one that includes vulnerability, surrender, self-valuing, steadiness, and a willingness to face, rather than run from, the worst of ourselves.

Compulsion is a state of isolation, one that includes self-absorption, invulnerability, low self-esteem, unpredictability, and fear that if we faced our pain, it would destroy us.

Love expands; compulsion diminishes.

Compulsion leaves no room for love—which is, in fact, why many people started eating: because when there was room for love, the people around us were not loving. The very purpose of compulsion is to protect ourselves from the pain associated with love.

It is my belief that we become compulsive because of wounds from our past and the decisions we made at that time about our self-worth—decisions about our capacity to love and whether, in fact, we deserve to be loved. Our mother goes away and we decide that we are unlovable. Our father is emotionally distant and we decide that we need too much. Someone we are close to dies and we decide that there is no reason to love anyone because it hurts too much at the end. We make decisions based on our pain and the limited choices we had at that time. We make decisions based on how we made sense of the wounds and what we did to protect ourselves from being more wounded in that environment. At the age of six or eleven or fifteen, we decide that love hurts and that we are unworthy or unlovable or too demanding, and we live the rest of our lives protecting ourselves from being hurt again. And there is no better protection than wrapping ourselves around a compulsion.

In any of my workshops, there are participants whose parents were alcoholic; there are participants whose parents died or left during childhood without a warning; there are participants who were beaten or raped; and there are participants whose losses, abandonments, and betrayals were subtler and had to do with any combination of unavailable fathers, possessive mothers, and families in which uncomfortable feelings were denied and repressed.

As children we have no resources, no power to make choices about our situations. We need our families for food, shelter, and love or else we will die. If we feel that the pain around us is too intense and we cannot leave or change it, we will shut it off. We will—and do—switch our pain to something less threatening: a compulsion.

As adults, it becomes our task to examine the decisions we made long ago about our self-worth, our capacity to love, and our willingness to be loved, for it is from these decisions that many of our beliefs about compulsion and love take root.

It is not possible to be obsessed with food or anything else and to be truly intimate with ourselves or another human being; there is simply not enough room. Yet all of us want intimacy. We all want to love and be loved.

Once we had no choice; now we do.

The decision to be intimate, like the decision to break free from compulsive eating, is not something that is given to you. Intimacy is not something that just happens between two people; it is a way of being alive. At every moment, we are choosing either to reveal ourselves or to protect ourselves, to value ourselves or to diminish ourselves, to tell the truth or to hide. To dive into life or to avoid it. Intimacy is making the choice to be connected to, rather than isolated from, our deepest truth at that moment.

In every workshop, I hear: "So when is the magic going to begin?"

And I say, "When you take the step, when you make the choice."

For those of us who are used to waiting for someone to bring love to our lives, the discovery that being intimate is a choice that we make at every moment is as close to magic as anyone ever comes.

CHAPTER

2

Being In and
Out of Control

The first time he invited me for dinner, Matt gave me a tour of his house. A tattered blue-and-white Indian-print couch was pushed against the wall in the living room. Next to it, with a leg missing, stood a green-and-mustard-yellow wooden parrot. An old-fashioned lamp with an amber-colored shade and white fringe stood next to the coffee table.

Adjoining the living room was the kitchen; I ran my fingertips across the surface of the table. "It's made of koa," Matt said. "A friend of mine made it. But c'mon upstairs," he said, pointing to a spiral wooden staircase in the foyer. I nodded. I wanted to see more: the paintings on his walls, the books he kept beside his bed, the row of colored bottles in his bathroom.

As I walked up the last step, I faced a room that I knew belonged to a woman. From the landing, I could see Chinese fans tacked to the wall and a painted pink-and-purple desk. "This was Lou Ann's study," he said, and we crossed the threshold.

I knew about Lou Ann. I knew that he and Lou Ann had been very much in love and that she had died when she was thirty-three of inoperable ovarian cancer during their fifth year together. I knew that he held her each time she received chemotherapy because they heard that the medicine would not be devastating if she was being loved while she received it. I knew that he moved into her hospital room with her, that she had gone into remission for a year, and that she died at home, surrounded by their friends. A year and a half had passed since her death.

Her desk, her ceramic clock, her fountain pens, were arranged as if she were coming back any minute. Shiny red earrings lay sprawled in a porcelain heart-shaped dish on a shelf. A leather-bound appointment book with a clear plastic marker in the shape of an airplane waited on her desk. Get-well cards were propped on the bookshelf, open so that the reader could be heartened by the message: "I love you, Lou. Fight hard. Get well. You can beat this. Love, Katherine"; "Take good care of yourself, Lulu. You are stronger than any cancer. You are a survivor. We are your friends. Call us anytime—Love, Daniel and Maggie."

The last card had a drawing of a clown on the front dressed in silver with black piping on his collar, black buttons on his suit, and ruby-red paint on his lips. The inside read: "Happy Valentine's Day to my true love. I love you forever, M."

In eighth grade, I was haunted by Miss Havisham in *Great Expectations*, who was deserted by her fiancé on her wedding day. For the rest of her life, she waits for him to return. She leaves the wedding cake, the presents, the decorations untouched. Rats live in the decayed frosting, cobwebs hang from the corners, and Miss Havisham, eighty years old and in a wedding dress, waits for her beloved's return.

In Lou Ann's room, I felt as if I had crossed the threshold into a twilight world in which the distinction between reality and fantasy, between grieving for the past and living in the present, between living and dying was muted.

Why were these cards still here a year and a half after she died? And her earrings and her appointment book? The leather on the appointment book was faded and worn, soft as pussy willow; a ring from a glass darkened the upper-right corner. I was torn between wanting to open it and see her handwriting, to read about the places she went, the people she met for lunch, and wanting to pretend that I hadn't seen it. How much of that date book did she use? Did she know she was going to die before the year ran out? And her earrings. Polished and rutilant. I liked them. The traces that were left of her after she was gone. In her desk drawer, I might find lists of things to buy: soap, shampoo, light bulbs; I might find photographs, notes from Matt: See you later, sweetheart, I went for a walk.

My breathing became shallow and tight. Each breath felt like a piece of glass shattering my chest. How could her earrings still be here when she was not? She had been only thirty-three. I wanted to know everything about her. And I wanted to forget that I ever heard her name. Or Matt's. Walk out of the room, down the steps, past the Indian-print couch and leave the house. Forever.

I didn't want to fall in love with a man who was in love with another woman—even if that other woman was dead. *Especially* if that other woman was dead. I could never measure up to her; she would be perfect in his memory. And I would always know that he was with me because he could not be with her. I wanted to be someone's first choice. I wanted a man to love me more than he had ever loved anyone else. Matt was getting in the way of how he was supposed to be.

I wanted to be in control—of my feelings, his feelings, the course of our relationship. In my dreams of meeting The One, I hadn't counted on being affected by death or grief. It was only our second date and the nature of our romance—its pace, its pitch, the kinds of feelings we would express with each other— was already skidding out of my carefully planned tracks. I wasn't in control and I knew it. I wasn't in control and I hated it.

Standing there in Lou Ann's room, the whooshing of cars in the street suddenly seemed too loud. I knew it was time to say something.

I looked at Matt. He was holding two small decks of cards in his hands.

"What are those?" I asked.

"They're called Oh cards," he said. "You choose one picture card and one words card and then you describe what the combination of the two cards means to you. Would you like to play?"

"Sure."

"Okay. I'll go first."

He picked a picture of a person just about to go down a slide and he picked a card that said, "Joy." He said, "I feel as if I've been climbing up a long staircase and now I'm ready to begin letting joy back into my life and play again. With you."

☙✕❧

For the first eight months that I knew Matt, he cried nearly every day. Sometimes he would cry as soon as he woke up in the morning. Sometimes he would cry when we were making love. One night we were at a dance and when "I'm So Excited" by the Pointer Sisters was played, he said he had to leave. "Lou Ann and I discovered the Pointer Sisters together," he said. "I can't dance to this one."

He would ask me to hold him when he cried. And I would. Hold him and rock him and stroke his forehead, his hair. He would talk about how emaciated she had become because of the cancer or he would remember the oxygen she needed at the very end and the shots he had to give her. He would speak of her playfulness before she got sick and her brightness and humor while she was sick. He told me that on their first Hawaiian trip they took hula lessons on a giant stage, and every time Lou Ann swished her hips, she knocked him off the stage. Soon they were laughing so hard they couldn't dance. He told me that Lou Ann was like a child; she made friends with everyone. If he was supposed to meet her at a restaurant and was twenty minutes late, she was already sitting at another table talking and laughing with a group of strangers. "She was dauntless," he said. "Everyone loved her, even the postman." When Lou Ann was doing her thesis on the mating behavior of polar bears, she went to the zoo every day to watch them. Within a week, Caesar, the ferocious male bear, was licking her hand.

In his office, Matt had a wall of pictures of Lou Ann. I counted them—twenty-three, twenty-four, twenty-five pictures in all. Lou Ann as a baby, Lou Ann in a bathing suit, Lou Ann kissing Matt, Lou Ann holding Matt's hand, both with pink streaks in their hair, both laughing. On his lamp was a note written in a woman's hand saying "Lou loves you." Next to the bottle of Ivory soap in the kitchen was a blue-and-white ceramic heart on which was engraved "Matt and Lou." In the shower stood her soap dish. In the cabinet stood her medicine. Her name and face were everywhere. Lou Ann. Lou Ann.

My feelings about loving and being loved by Matt while he grieved for Lou Ann vacillated tremendously. I wanted him in my life. I was moved by his tears and his pain, and it felt important, *I* felt important, when he was vulnerable with me. I knew that I could not imagine what it was like for him to watch helplessly as her body grew weak, her hair fell out, and death, like a siren, called to relieve her. I was already beginning to feel that if anything happened to Matt, I would be destroyed. ("Everyone's worst fear," Sara said. "It's obvious that he is a man who can make a commitment, Geneen. If you are patient with him, it will be well worth it.")

But I was falling madly in love with this man; I was ecstatic, I was radiant, I was anything but sad. I felt that life had showered us with blessings; he felt that life had stolen his most precious treasure. I felt that I had met the love of my life; he felt that his had already died. I felt that making love with him brought me to the place in my body, beneath my bones, behind my eyes, where my questions became answers; he felt that making love brought him closer to endless sadness. I felt stronger and more alive than ever; he felt that a part of him had died with Lou Ann and he wasn't sure that he could ever be fully alive again. Or that he wanted to.

I wanted my love to be enough to heal him—and it wasn't. I wanted to be the only woman in his life—and I wasn't.

❃✖❃

When Lou Ann had been dead for almost three years, Matt and I went to a grief counselor. I was convinced that Matt was prolonging his grief and that he was using it to keep me at a distance. I was tired of hearing about the part of him that died when Lou Ann did, tired of looking at the picture on his study wall of the two of them locked in an embrace. I was ready for him to be done.

Looking at me, the counselor said, "You really want this to happen in your time, don't you?" The counselor said, "You would really like to orchestrate what happens and when it happens." The counselor said, "It sounds as if you believe that if Matt loved you, he wouldn't miss Lou Ann."

Yes to all of the above.

Yes to my belief that I can control the beginnings and endings of almost anything. Yes to my belief that if things don't happen the way I want them to, my first reaction is that I am doing it wrong, have done something wrong, can do something to make it better.

No to the helplessness and terror of being out of control. I tried that once. It didn't work.

In my childhood house the most frequent sounds were doors slamming, raised voices. My mother hit my brother and me, would back us into corners of the living room, the kitchen. I remember standing in a corner, holding my arms in front of my face so that she wouldn't grab my hair, scratch my eyes. I was frightened that she would break me.

My father, elusive and smiling, danced through it all. He gave me presents, called me pussycat, and told me that he loved me. He left for work early in the morning and returned late at night. He left in the middle of fights with my mom; from my bedroom,

I could hear them screaming, could hear the front door slam, could hear my mother yelling, "Don't leave, you bastard," could hear the car start. As the sound of the engine faded, my mother would slam doors, throw plates, cry. And I would wait. Wait for my father to come home, wait for my mother to stop screaming, wait for it to be safe to come out.

At twelve, I made a decision that if things in my family were going to work, I was going to have to make them work.

At twelve, I made a list in my diary. I called it: "Things I Can Do to Make My Mom Happy." This is the list:

1. clean my room
2. bring her breakfast in bed
3. say nice things
4. don't get mad or call anyone stupid
5. don't ask questions

At the end of each day, I would check the things I had done on the list. I would star the things I could do tomorrow. Keeping the list gave me the feeling that I was accomplishing something. It made me feel as if I were in control.

Every night I had the same dream: I was standing in the middle of my room pushing hard against the walls which were crumbling. I couldn't let go, not even for a minute. If I did, the walls would fall down, the house would crumble. And so would I.

When friends asked me to sleep at their house, I said no. I told them I didn't feel well. I couldn't tell them that my job was at home, holding up the walls. I didn't want to join committees that met after school; I didn't want to spend a night away; I didn't want to come home to a house that was falling down.

My friend Robert told me that from the time he was in third grade to the time he was in seventh grade, his mother had four nervous breakdowns. They began by her staying in bed all day for two weeks. She stopped talking, stopped eating, stopped sleeping. He would come home from school and go to his room and draw pictures, bring them to her. He would make toast and Lipton's tea and carry it to her on a white wicker tray. He would take a bite of toast, then hand her the plate and say, "Now you do it, Mom." He believed that he could make his mother well, that her health was in his control.

Maggie, the therapist I see, said, "You can't make anyone leave, Geneen. In the same way that you can't make anyone stay. They stay or they leave because of decisions they make, because of reasons that have to do with them, not because of something you do or don't do on a particular day."

I didn't believe her.

❀✖❀

Control. It's a word that compulsive eaters hear often. On every diet, in every meeting, in every book. We learn very early that a fundamental part of us—our hunger—is out of control. We learn that if we are to look and live like normal human beings, we must be forever watchful of the wild hunger inside. We live in fear of food, in fear of chocolate and sour cream and cinnamon rolls, while believing that if only we can get that part of us under control, everything else will fall into place. But this belief is only a smoke screen that distracts us from the core issue: the areas in which we never were and never will be in control. The areas that have to do with loving and being loved.

When we become intimate with someone else, we lose control. We lose control of how long they stay or if they leave, how they feel about us, how we feel about things they do or say. We lose control of the effect that loving them has on our lives. We become vulnerable to loss, pain, death.

A sixty-year-old woman is sitting in the back of the room during a workshop I am leading. It is September, it is very hot, and the air conditioning has broken. When she raises her hand, I move closer and notice that she is huddled in a mink coat.

"If I don't eat," she says, "I am going to perish."

"How much do you weigh?" I ask.

"I am afraid to tell you."

"Sometimes saying things out loud is helpful," another participant whispers.

"I weigh seventy pounds," she answers.

Her eyes are dark globes of misery, her cheekbones are flat planes of bone that extend so far from her face that they seem unrelated to her cheeks.

"I stopped eating twenty years ago."

"What happened twenty years ago?" I ask.

"My daughter died of leukemia. I thought I would perish."

Rather than experience the loss of control that loving brings, many of us choose to feel out of control about something that is within our control: the food we eat—or don't eat.

The issue of control—over our actions, our feelings, other people's behavior—is central to any compulsion. The lack of control is what compulsion seems to be about. A workshop participant says, "When I buy a box of chocolates, I eat two pieces and then I put the rest of the box in a drawer. I go back to my study and after a few minutes I hear the chocolate calling to me. 'Marni,' it sings, 'Marni, come get me.' I swear, the chocolate has a voice. Oh, I know it doesn't really have vocal chords, but it calls to me and I answer. I have to. In that moment, I feel as if I have no choice."

When I binged, I felt as if I were possessed. I wanted to be thin, wanted to love, wanted to create, but the binge wanted to destroy, ravage, wipe out. When I binged, I didn't care about anyone else; there were times when if anything or anyone was standing in the way between me and food, I felt as if I could have mowed it down. Killed someone. And when I stopped bingeing and surveyed the damage—the food I had eaten, the urgency with which I had eaten it, the utter disregard for anyone I had seen before or during the binge—I was frightened. The binge seemed to have a mind of its own, a voice of its own, a will of its own.

I learned to be frightened of my binges in the same way that as a child, I was frightened of my mother. I saw my mother as someone who lost her temper and for the moment or the hour or the day was like a tornado tearing up all that stood in her way. Strong hands, red face, pulsing veins. There was no telling when she would hit me; there was no predicting what would make her angry. There was no such thing as being safe. Which, years later, is exactly how I felt around food. Like many people with whom I work, I transferred the terror that was outside of me—my childhood terror—to a terror that was inside of me. When we are compulsive about food, we recreate familiar feelings of being out of control, being frightened, being frustrated, being helpless, but this time the feelings are encompassed by a tiny—and much safer—radius: the food that goes in our mouths, the weight that goes on our bodies.

⊛✖⊛

Last month in San Diego, a woman in a workshop said that food was her drug and that she was helpless to do anything about it. And that relieved her. "It's good to know that food is out of my control," she said.

Well, I don't believe that.

I believe she believes that, and I believe it's comforting and familiar to believe that, but I don't believe that it's true.

What I believe is that at one time many things *were* out of control and that quite probably some of those things were very painful. Maybe they were devastating. Let's say that this woman's father was an alcoholic. Or let's say that her brother abused her sexually. Let's say that as a child, for whatever reasons, she was not valued, not listened to, not treated with respect and dignity. And that being a child, she was absolutely out of control of her situation. It makes sense that as an adult she would try to control or try to avoid what she believed responsible for that pain. It makes sense that as an adult, she would find those feelings of being out of control so familiar and so compelling that she would recreate them, but this time in a situation in which she was ultimately in control and therefore would not be vulnerable to the decisions, desires, or moods of anyone who could hurt her, who could prevail over her childhood terror.

❃✗❃

We all have broken hearts. Every single one of us has had our heart broken at least once—in our families, from the loss or betrayal of a parent. Some had their hearts broken over and over again in terrible ways. When the heart of a child is broken, something inexpressible—and up to that moment whole and un-questioned—snaps. And nothing is ever the same. We spend the rest of our lives trying to minimize the hurt or pretend that it didn't happen, trying to protect ourselves from its happening again, trying to get someone to love us the way we, as that child, needed to be loved. We spend the rest of our lives eating or drinking or smoking or working so that we never have to go back there again. Never have to feel the unbearable pain of our broken hearts.

I see it in the workshop participants. They walk into the room expectant, hopeful, protected. They want me to prove to them that what I say is true, will make a difference in their lives. They are angry; they have been holding on for so long, waiting for someone to provide the key that will open their lives and allow them to become who they dream they can be. We talk about patterns of intimacy, we talk about patterns of compulsive eating, but it is not until we talk about and they allow themselves to feel the pain of childhood that their faces change and they begin to breathe. From the front of the room, the moment of change is almost palpable. Their eyes become soft; their shoulders drop, and I am no longer the focus of attention. For the moment, at least, they have exactly what they need: they have touched the bottom of themselves. They've reached in to the time and place when their hearts were broken.

They raise their hands. One woman shares her story:

"I'm the oldest of six children. My father's father was a severe alcoholic and his mother was a child abuser. Although my father wasn't actively drinking when I was growing up, he was very rigid with us. There was a lot of verbal abuse, not so much physical abuse—at least that I can remember.

"My mom was sickly and away in the hospital a lot, so I became a caretaker at a very early age. I was cooking Sunday dinners for all of us when I was eight years old. This was the only time I received any praise from Daddy, so I did more and more cooking, cleaning, babysitting—waiting like a dry sponge for something to soak up and make me feel useful, valid, like I deserved to be alive.

"In the guided fantasy* you led, I went back to a time in my life when I was very scared. My mother was addicted to tranquilizers. She was being hospitalized and I was waiting to say goodbye to her on my way to school one morning. She had packed a suitcase and I was sitting on the couch next to it. It was open and I was looking at what she was bringing with her. I was eleven or twelve and I found pills sewn into her bras. I found them in an empty perfume bottle—I found them everywhere. And I told my father. Well, she looked at me as if I'd burned her, and I was sent off to school.

"On the way home, I stopped into our church to cry. No

---

* As part of Breaking Free workshops, participants take part in one or a few eyes-closed guided fantasies whose purpose is to help them get in touch with events and feelings of which they may not be consciously aware.

one was there. I was so alone. I thought my mother was going to die. I thought she was going to leave us, that she wanted to leave us and I couldn't stand how awful it was. I felt like my body was going to break in a million pieces. And I knew I had to go home and take care of the other kids, make supper.

"While I sat there, a wedding party came in for rehearsal, talking and laughing until the bride spotted me in the front row. She turned to the priest and said very loudly, "Who *is* that? What's she doing here?" and I ran out the side door and cried all the way home.

"As part of the fantasy, you said, 'Now, you as the adult can go to that child and comfort her. Let her know that she is loved.' And I rebelled inside. My adult didn't want to do that. I can remember feeling something to the effect of 'If you give me one more person to take care of, I'm going to crack.' I've been taking care of people since I was five years old. I'm now thirty-five. I have three young children under six; I'm in my second alcoholic marriage—'recovering,' however, but what a struggle to reach a 'normal' point over ten years. And I'm tired. I want a turn to be irresponsible, childlike, needy instead of needed. As soon as I begin feeling this, I start eating, bingeing because I feel selfish and eating is the only way I know to give to myself and let myself be out of control.

"I've gone to counseling for two years, Al-Anon for one and a half. I was beginning to feel like I was breaking free, but as soon as I get back in touch with that child, I start bingeing again."

❧✖❧

A child finds pills sewn into her mother's bras. Her drug-addicted mother is so involved in her own world, so glazed with her own pain that she cannot possibly pay attention to the children. Her father, rigid and abusive, is the child's only source of love. She learns that she will be praised—praise being all she knows of love—when she takes care of the five other children. She marries two men and repeats her role of caretaker because it is the only way she knows to "soak up" love. And she takes care of herself by eating, only by eating. Indulging herself in food the way she wanted to be indulged in love. But her eating precipitates an onslaught of guilt. She feels selfish when she eats, and being selfish, she learned very young, does not get her the love she feels dry without. Wanting to be loved, but also wanting to validate and meet her own needs, she maintains control in every area of her life but eating. And she continues to believe that at her very core, something is terribly wrong with her.

❀✖❀

I was eleven the year my mother called me into her room to tell me she was getting a divorce. I had known for years that my parents were very unhappy, and I had been praying nightly that they would stay together. Kneeling at the side of my bed, I would say, "Please bless Mommy and Daddy and Howard and please, God, don't let them get a divorce." I didn't know where I would go, what would happen to me. I thought that I would get sent to court and that I would have to stand before a judge, with my mother on one side and my father on the other side of the courtroom. I thought that the judge would tell me that I had to choose which one I loved best, which one I wanted to be with. And I didn't want to have to make that choice. I believed that if I went with my father, my mother wouldn't love me any more, but that if I went with my mother, my father would still love me. I wanted to go with my father because he was easier to live with and because I felt loved by him, but I didn't want to lose my mother.

On the day that my mother told me she wanted a divorce, I started to cry. "What will I do? Where will I go?" I asked.

"All you think about is yourself," she said. "Don't you ever think about anyone else's feelings?"

I stopped crying immediately, ashamed. "I'm sorry, Mom. I didn't mean it."

"Go to your room," she said.

And I did. It was a Thursday night; I watched "Bewitched." I stared at the curves in the plaster ceiling. When I heard the key turn in the front door, I bounded down the stairs and met my father as he was taking off his coat.

"Mom says you're getting a divorce."

"We're getting a *what?*" he said, laughing.

"A divorce. Why are you laughing?"

Without answering me, he walked up the stairs and opened the door to their bedroom.

The next day, my mother didn't say—and I didn't ask—another word about it.

When my mother got angry at me, she told me I was selfish. And that meant that I thought about myself first instead of thinking about her or my brother. Being selfish was the same as being bad. Being selfish must be the reason she didn't love me, I thought. I grew up with the belief that I wouldn't be loved if I thought about myself.

Eating was a way to secretly give to myself. When I ate three packages of orange cupcakes with the white squiggly line across the middle, I didn't have to ask anyone. No one could see that I wanted them—or anything—for myself.

One afternoon I was walking past my parents' bedroom and I heard my brother crying. He was talking to my father: "I bought a package of Hostess Sno-Balls with my own money—one for me and one for Geneen—and now they are gone. You ate them both, didn't you?"

"I probably did, Howard," my father said, "and I'm sorry. I didn't know you were saving them."

I tiptoed into my room. It took twenty years for me to tell my brother that I, and not my father, had eaten both of them.

I was ashamed that I was selfish, I was ashamed that I ate so much, that I hid food in my pajamas, coats, pockets. I was ashamed of so many things, but most of all, I was ashamed of who I was.

At an early age, I learned to be out of control around food and in control around people—which is, in fact, the trade-off that many of us who are compulsive about food make. Everything that we believe we are *not allowed* to do in our lives—with people, in our work—we allow ourselves with food: We eat the biggest one, we take the best for ourselves, we take more than we need, we spend money, we don't think about others. We allow ourselves to have exactly what we want. As for the rest of our lives, we are always on a diet of restricted feelings. Because at some age each of us learned that to be loved, we could not reveal ourselves. To be loved, we could not ask for what we wanted.

We began defining love, then, as something elusive, something that we could only get if we pretended we were not who we were. We learned at an early age to mold ourselves into our image of the perfect child—the one we imagined would get all the love that we, in our imperfections, were not receiving. When we ate, we felt both victorious and desperate—victorious because it was our way, sometimes our only way, of being ourselves, and desperate because being ourselves seemed to take us further and further away from what we wanted more than anything else: to be loved. We practiced—and became masterful at—being someone else. But underneath the wrapping was an awful knowledge that who we were, who we really were, was not lovable.

Every time we eat compulsively, we reinforce the belief that the only way we can have what we want is to give it to ourselves, that unless we are in control of our nourishment we will go hungry. At the same time, and precisely because it is a way to give to ourselves, compulsive eating triggers old messages that we are bad for having needs and especially bad if we satisfy them. It has come to symbolize all that is wrong with us: that we have needs and that we have the arrogance to actually provide for these needs ourselves. Every time we use food compulsively, we trigger the hopelessness of learning that meeting our needs means we will never, ever be loved.

In this context, compulsive eating is an affirmation of the human spirit. It is our way of saying, "You cannot beat me down. Although I am vulnerable and believe I need your love, although I might change what I say and what I do to please you, there is a part of me that will remain intact no matter what. This part of me cannot be bought or sold; it knows it is worthy of love and pleasure and fulfillment. This is the part of me that eats."

And that is true.

When, as children or adults, we live in environments in which we learn that when we express our humanness we will not be loved, we adapt. We learn how to pretend we are someone other than who we are, but all the while, a strong voice shouts no, and because we don't hear it, it uses food as its language. Being controlled precipitates being out of control . . . of something: food, work, sex, drugs. It also precipitates a need to remain in control of what we believe we will not receive unless we control the receiving. Of love, for instance.

❀✖❀

Six months ago, on my suggestion, Matt and I planned a weekend trip to a bed-and-breakfast inn. Three days before we were to leave, Matt told me that a good friend of his had called and invited him to his fortieth birthday party in Chicago. "I'd like to go," Matt said. "Sounds great," I said. "When is it?" "It's the evening of the last day of our trip. I'd need to leave early that morning."

My body stiffened. I told him that it wasn't okay with me. Through tears, I told him he was always changing plans we made and that this was supposed to be our special time together and I couldn't believe that he wanted to cut one day from three days to go to the party of a friend he hadn't seen in a year.

His body stiffened. He told me that it wasn't okay with him that it wasn't okay with me. He told me that while it was true about his always changing plans, he liked to be flexible and didn't see anything wrong with it. He told me that I always had to have it my way, otherwise I got angry and where was the room for him, anyway?

That fight was one of our basic fights: I make plans based on what Matt and I decide, then he wants to change the plans and I feel hurt, let down, angry.

I remember when I was in eleventh grade and practicing to get my driver's license. My mother and I would set a time to go out driving and I would go home from school and wait for her. About a half hour after she was supposed to show, the phone would ring. She would tell me that she couldn't make it. If I reacted, she would get angry. She would tell me that she needed time alone and that I always wanted things my way.

During that year, my boyfriend Sheldon died of cancer. I spent days writing his name on everything—my arms, my legs, my homework. I cried myself to sleep and I cried throughout the day. Mr. Benson, my typing teacher, left a box of tissues on my desk during his Monday/Wednesday/Friday class. My friend Carolyn and her parents were going on a cruise during winter break and invited me to join them. I wanted to go. My mother was going to Florida and invited me to go with her. She told me that either way, the cruise or Florida, was fine with her.

It seemed to me that if I gave up going on the cruise to be with my mother, she would certainly realize how much I loved her and wanted her attention. The unspoken assumption I made was that if I wound myself around her, she would wind herself around me.

If I give up what I want to do, then you will give up what you want to do.

Control.

Underneath the "if I give up what I want to do" is the belief that I am not allowed to/cannot do what I want to do. Taking care of myself is wrong. Having needs is bad. Providing for them is worse. A loving person thinks of the other first. A loving person takes the smallest cookie. This means that if we are ever to feel loved, we must rely on someone else for that love. And as soon as we begin relying on others to fill us, we feel the need, the urgency, to control what they do and say; the reflection of ourselves in their eyes becomes critical. They must love us a particular way, say things in a particular manner. They must love us the way we would love ourselves if only we were allowed. They must become what we define as loving so that we will know we are loved. They must do everything our parents didn't.

If we believe that we don't deserve and therefore cannot give appreciation, respect, and tenderness to ourselves, then we will try to get these things from others—even if we have to humiliate ourselves in the process. We give for the purpose of receiving. We do things for the effect they will have. We try to manipulate or connive or control others into giving to us whatever we believe we cannot give to ourselves. We become what is commonly referred to as "controlling."

Matt wasn't playing by the rules. And it took many many fights to discover what exactly those rules were.

For a year and a half after we met, I didn't make plans to do anything without him on a night when I could be with him. Because I wanted him to do the same. Because I didn't want to be left. Because the only way I knew to get what I wanted was to give up what I wanted and hope that someone else would give it to me. And what I wanted was to know, with a conviction as unshakable as Sally's redwood tree with the trunk that is twelve feet around, with the leaves that cut clouds in two—what I wanted was to know once and for all that yes, Geneen, yes, you have a right to need, to want, to ask, to have. You don't have to be ashamed any longer. You can bloom now, it's all right.

For many years, I thought that being thin would give that to me. It didn't. Then I thought that having books published would provide it. They didn't. But then I realized that of course, things can't do that, but people can. When I met and fell in love with Matt, my unspoken expectation was that he would save me from myself. From my self-hatred, from the anguish I felt at being who I was, from my anguish about all the things I was that I didn't want to be.

Matt wasn't playing by the rules. He could not save me from myself, from my experience of getting hit when I asked for what I wanted, from my unwillingness to begin taking care of myself in the present moment.

⊛✖⊛

I received this letter yesterday:

> I am a nineteen-year-old college student. I have always been protected from the emotions and sensations connected to intimacy because I first believed I was overweight and then I actually was overweight during junior high and high school.
>
> I lost forty pounds last summer and arrived at college ready for a new life. I ran into an old friend the first night that I was at school and we ended up kissing.
>
> I enjoyed it. I liked him. I liked being close to him. Abruptly, I ended our contact even though I liked it. I was so confused after that. We had another encounter a couple of weeks later. I finally felt full with real pleasure, but at a point before sex, I stopped him.
>
> I don't know why *I won't let myself go*. [italics mine] I started to gain weight when what I really wanted was human contact. Contact that I deprived myself of. Maybe after my many experiences with food, I thought that I wouldn't be able to get enough.
>
> Over the next three months, I gained thirty pounds.
>
> I cannot stop thinking that I am lonely. That all I want is love and closeness. I cannot stop filling myself with food. Just as I want intimacy the most, I feel the least worthy of it because now I am

fat and unattractive. I am also protected. Please, Geneen, can you help me?

Can I help? Only if she is willing to examine why she is frightened of being close, for it is not that her weight makes her feel fat and unattractive but that being close and feeling real pleasure are terrifying to her and so she uses her weight to keep herself at a distance. As long as she is feeling fat, she has an excuse not to be intimate. She can blame her loneliness on her weight. With no extra weight, she would have no barriers between herself and another person.

The question remains: Why is she frightened of being close?
. What were her early experiences of being loved and loving? What happened that made her so frightened?

We become frightened of intimacy *because our intimate experiences were frightening*, not because we are incapable of loving. If we are ever to deeply love ourselves—or anyone else—we must first examine why we are frightened. We must go back to the beginning, reexperience (or perhaps allow ourselves to feel for the first time, since when those feeling first arose, we pushed them away) the rage, hurt, fear, betrayal, loss of what it was like to be the child we were, a child in our family of origin. But this time, with a support system—a therapist, friends, a peer-support group focused on our particular issues—that will validate, absorb, love us through our feelings instead of deny, ignore, or punish us because of them. Then and only then can we heal and move on.

❀✖❀

A refrigerator cannot break my heart.

But Matt can.

At least that is what I have believed until now. I have treated him as if he could snap me in two, as if I had to be in charge of making sure that he didn't. As if my job were to keep the walls from crumbling. As if my job were to keep his walls from crumbling so that mine could remain intact.

As children, we believe that we are in control of the pain in our lives, because the truth—being helpless in the midst of crumbling walls—is too much to handle; it is overwhelming. If we had allowed ourselves to feel the reality of the situation, we might have been unable to walk, talk, or otherwise function. We might have literally lost our minds. So we take it upon ourselves to make Sunday dinners, to feed our mothers toast from white wicker trays; we give ourselves the illusion of power in an otherwise powerless environment.

However, what served us well as children hinders our growth as adults. If we continue to believe, as I have, that we can be in control of the beginnings and endings of things, we will be constantly frustrated, disappointed, and confused. We will not have soul-satisfying love in our lives. By operating under the illusion of power that was never, and can never be, ours, we will totally miss the opportunity of owning the power that as children we did not have and as adults we *do* have: that of taking good and loving care of ourselves, making ourselves happy. It is not our job to be in charge of anyone but ourselves.

❧✕❧

As a teenager and through my twenties, when I dreamed of being with a man, I saw myself being held by him, I saw him comforting me. I saw myself being healed.

That isn't what has happened. In fact, it is quite the opposite. Being loved by Matt heightens the ways in which I already felt complete and exacerbates the emptiness.

Being loved in the present brings up all the ways in which we were not loved in the past. No amount of love in the present, not a single person, not ten thousand people loving us all at once, can make up for or take away the pain of the betrayals of the past, just as bingeing today for deprivation in the past or for deprivation to come does not make up for the many times we said to ourselves, "You can't have that, you're fat and you're ugly." The only insurance against repeating the pain in the past is to allow ourselves to feel it fully and release it in the present.

We will never be children again. No one, nothing can ever hurt us that way again. Only a child is defenseless and totally reliant on those around her to protect, affirm, and love her.

When we allow our bodies or our weight to interfere with the quality of intimacy in our lives, when we feel too fat to have our thighs or our bellies stroked, when we feel too ugly to be seen with the lights on, we are trying to protect ourselves from being hurt. Again. But the hurt we are protecting ourselves from is not in the present. Nor is it in the future. We are trying to protect ourselves from feeling a hurt that has nothing to do with our lives now; over and over, for the rest of our lives, we try to protect ourselves from feeling our past, and in so doing we never allow ourselves to claim the present.

☻✖☻

Matt and I disassembled Lou Ann's room. First we took the Chinese fans from the wall. We traced our fingers along the delicate lines of the gold trees. Then we picked up her ceramic clock, her fountain pens, her earrings in the heart-shaped dish. Matt said he would like the clock for his office; he laid it gently by the door. We threw the pens in the wastebasket, put the earrings in a box for Lou Ann's mother. When we opened the appointment book to the clear plastic marker, we saw that it was clipped to the month of April. Lou Ann died on April 18. There was a list of things she wanted to do: call Dougie, say affirmations, breathe easy with the oxygen. Matt's tears spilled onto the page, blurring the word "oxygen." He asked me to hold him for a moment, and when I did, he sobbed. When he stopped, we continued to take things apart, put things away. The desk, the shelves, the cards. In three and a half hours, the room was packed in a trunk and three boxes. "Let's put these in the closet," Matt said. "I don't want to banish Lou Ann to the garage." Three months later, at his suggestion, we moved the boxes and the trunk outside, to the garage.

As for me, I am in the process of taking my childhood room apart. And with each feeling I touch, cry about, and put away, each memory of fear, each experience of loss,
the walls
are crumbling.
And I am setting myself free.

CHAPTER

3

The Comfort
of Suffering

When I introduced myself to Matt, I knew I was introducing myself to a man whose lover had died of cancer. I knew because he had told the story when I heard his presentation the day before. I knew that having a relationship with him would not be easy. But I wasn't looking for easy.

I invent drama where there is none. I feel most at home with chaos. I thrive on intensity.

I get frantic, never concerned.

I get ecstatic, never glad.

I get miserable, never unhappy.

And I have refined the art of suffering.

Being with someone whose lover has died of cancer is high drama. The stuff of soap operas. Like Dr. Kildare in "Tyger, Tyger."

When I was in high school, I saw Yvette Mimieux and Richard Chamberlain in a special two-part Dr. Kildare show, in which Yvette was a blond California surfer-girl with grand mal epilepsy and Richard was the loving handsome doctor who was called in to rescue her. Despite their ensuing love, she continued to ride the waves and eventually, during a seizure and against the background words of William Blake's poem "Tyger, Tyger," Yvette died.

The combination of passion and grief enthralled me. I decided that I wanted to *be* Yvette Mimieux. With her hair, her body, and her style, I would be so beautiful that I would never be lonely again. I would be popular with girls and desired by boys. My phone would ring constantly. I would have a laugh that chimed, a smile that was irresistible. I wouldn't have time for the boys in my class, the ones who were tormenting me about my round face, because men like Richard Chamberlain would fall in love with me. And if not Richard Chamberlain, I reasoned, then certainly the usher at the Squire movie theater, my current heartthrob: Mike Howard.

Yvette Mimieux was a blond, willowy surfer. I was a brown-haired, chunky tenth-grader. I sprayed Sun-In in my hair to make it blond, not realizing that the peroxide would turn the brown color to luminescent green. I went on a prunes-and-meatball diet to become willowy. I posted a magazine photograph of Yvette on the refrigerator so that every time I reached for ice cream, I would see her 5'7" legs on her 5'8" body. I wanted those legs. And that was a problem. On my 5'2" body, my legs played a minimal role. It's not that they weren't substantial—my brother called me Thunder Thighs—it's just that they were very short.

After two weeks of green hair and short legs, I decided that I was being superficial and petty. I didn't need blond hair and long legs to be Yvette Mimieux; I needed to have epilepsy. Grand mal epilepsy. That was, after all, what had brought Dr. Kildare into her life. That was what made their love so precious and what caused her to die a glamorous death. Her eyes rolling upward as she rode a wave, Dr. Kildare arriving on the scene a moment too late. Her limp body being dragged from the ocean while his face glistened with tears of anguish. I wanted someone to care about me the way he cared about her.

So I practiced having epileptic seizures. Practiced rolling my eyes upward and falling to the floor without cracking my skull. I set the stage for my performance. I told my friends Claudia and

Bunny that I had epilepsy; I asked Bunny to see *Khartoum* with me at the Squire theater. When Mike saw us, he walked over to say hello, and in the middle of discussing our social studies exam, I rolled my eyes and fell gracefully to the floor. He picked me up and carried me to a chair. "She just found out that she has grand mal epilepsy," Bunny whispered to Mike. He grabbed the cardboard from a discarded Baby Ruth bar and put it in my mouth so that I wouldn't swallow my tongue. But after two more seizures, Mike's mother forbade him to see me again.

In eleventh and twelfth grades, my friends and I would spend evenings together making phony phone calls to our boyfriends. Susan would call my boyfriend and say, "Have you seen Geneen tonight?" Since I was sitting next to Susan at that moment, he would answer no. Then Susan would say, "I'm so worried about her. She left here very upset and I'm concerned that she's been in some kind of accident. Would you call me if you hear from her?"

We hoped that the prospect of our imminent death would fan our boyfriends' ardor. When they were faced with the possibility of losing us, we were certain they would realize how much they loved us.

❧✖❧

For the first six months that I traveled as a Breaking Free workshop leader, I would ask my friend Lew to have lunch with me on the day before my departure. We would drive the Pacific Coast Highway to the Davenport Café. If it was winter, we would scan the ocean for the spouts of the gray whales. If it was spring, we would count the variety of wildflowers growing on the hillside and comment on the calla lilies that grew in a perfect circle outside the café. As Lew was taking his last bite of dessert, I would say, "I'm leaving tomorrow to do a workshop. If the plane crashes and you never see me again, what would you wish you had said to me today?"

57

The first time I asked the question, Lew looked startled. "Oh, Geneen," he said, "I can't *imagine* the plane crashing."

"But it's possible," I answered. "It's always possible. You have to live as if you're going to die tomorrow and not leave anything unfinished. Do you want me to know anything that you haven't told me?"

"I love you," he said. "It has meant so much to me to be this close. I haven't had a friend like you in such a long time. You have kept after me, you haven't let me get away with not being in touch, and I feel good about the commitment I've made to us."

His eyes, the color of wet shale, filled with tears as he reached to clasp my hands in his. "I would miss you so if you died."

Thinking of the plane fuselage in flames, my family searching the wreck for any signs of me, my gold lamé shoes, my heart-shaped glasses, I cried, too.

"I don't want to die," I whispered to Lew.

The second time we went to the Davenport Café, I ordered the avocado-and-cheese sandwich on whole wheat toast and Lew ordered the lasagne. As I took the last bite of his pecan pie, I asked him if there was anything he would want me to know if the plane crashed tomorrow and I died.

His eyes misted like morning fog on the beach. "I love you and I'm glad you are my friend. You've been wonderful."

The third time we went to the Davenport Café, I ordered the avocado-and-cheese sandwich and he ordered the scampi. As I was picking the chocolate chips out of his dessert cookie, I asked him if there was anything he needed to say to me, since I might die the next day.

"Three things," he said. "Number one: Could you please leave me your record collection? Number two: Wherever you go when you die, look for me in about thirty years. I'll be wearing a red rose on my tuxedo jacket. And number three: You can't live like this, Geneen. You aren't going to die tomorrow. It's too much, too intense. It puts a frame around every thought, every feeling, and it doesn't allow you to give yourself or the people around you any slack."

I wanted to live as if I were going to die the next day. The combination of passion and grief enthralled me.

❸✖❸

When I had known Matt for ten months, I went to the doctor for advice about the pain in my right side and the clusters of itchy rashes that accompanied it. He told me that I had shingles. He told me that shingles was caused by a virus but stress was thought to trigger it and I would probably be in pain for three months to a year.

The pain felt like switchblades ripping through my bones. I wanted to hurl myself into a wall, bury myself in concrete, to stop it. I was furious that I was sick. I didn't want to give up writing, dancing, being outside, leading workshops. I didn't want to be like Lou Ann. And yet I wanted to *be* Lou Ann. If I was sick like Lou Ann, then maybe he would love me the way he loved Lou Ann. With urgency and passion. With the knowledge that I might not be there forever so why hold anything—any love, any affection—back.

When I talked to Sara about the way Matt must have loved Lou Ann, she would say, "But she died, Geneen. She died. You're *alive*. His love for her was mixed with sadness and fear. Do you really want him to love you that way? Wouldn't you rather he love you from a joyful place within himself?"

Yes, but . . .

Wouldn't that mean he'd love me less?

Wouldn't that mean he'd pay less attention to me?

Wouldn't that mean we'd be like those couples who once loved all the little things about each other—the curve of the neck, the space between the teeth—and over the years grew to hate those very things they once loved?

I don't want to be one of those restaurant couples eating dinner in stony silence.

"I'd rather be sick," I tell Sara.

"You're saying that you would rather die for love than live through the fights, the colds, the banalities of daily life?"

No. I would rather die than live like my mother and father.

She drank. Dewar's on the rocks with a twist of lemon. He said nothing. She took drugs. Amphetamines to lose weight, barbiturates to fall asleep. He said nothing. She screamed. At him, at us, at the dog. He said nothing. She pleaded. Am I pretty? she would ask him. He said nothing. She walked in the house at four-thirty in the morning, clothes rumpled, lipstick smeared. He said nothing. At Thanksgiving dinner she threw a plate of stuffing in his face. During a fight with my brother, she hurled a knife across the room. When she was angry at me, she dragged me into my room by the hair. He said nothing. On Sundays, when we went to the Steak Joint on Bleecker Street, they would eat in deadly silence.

My mother was dying for love and killing everything in sight. My father said nothing.

The life I knew as a child was either high-pitched emotional frenzy or absolutely still. My mother was in the house and miserable—or no one was home. There seemed to be only two choices: live in chaos or be abandoned.

Rather than relive my childhood, I have recreated my mother's life—constantly upping the ante in a desperate attempt to get my partner's attention.

Even when I already have it.

❧✖❧

As a way of introducing themselves to each other, I ask workshop participants to design a name tag for themselves. In one corner of the paper, they write what they imagine their lives would be like if food were not a problem. Many of them write "boring."

When I question them about it, they say that they would not know what to do with their time. They say life would be flat and without excitement.

They say: "When I am grabbing for food in that urgent way—you know the way I mean, when I can't get enough and it's a matter of life and death whether I get that piece of chocolate in my mouth this minute—it's part of a manic, exhilarating high. I *like* that high. I like feeling so alive. Without the pushing and pulling that takes place around food, life would be calmer, but I think it would be boring, too."

And they say: "Gaining and losing weight, always being on a diet is like being on an emotional roller coaster. Some days I am thrilled and other days I feel like hell, but at least I *feel* something. I can't imagine what my life would be like if I didn't have food to occupy my time."

There is nothing boring about being a compulsive eater. You are either hating yourself because you are too fat, giddy with the prospect of being thinner, or ready to rip yourself apart when you binge. Chaos, intensity, and drama are normal in the day-to-day life of a compulsive eater. Suffering is a way of being in the world.

It is as if we act out the parent-child relationship inside us when we eat. If what we heard or thought we heard as children was that we were bad and therefore deserved what was coming to us, we act that out by eating until we are so uncomfortable we can't move. It is not uncommon for someone who is not a compulsive eater to think it unfathomable to eat so much that she would be miserable. Why would anyone want to eat that much? What's the point? The point is not the taste or the texture or the smell of food; overeating is a means to give ourselves what we believe we deserve.

Compulsive eating is a dramatic restaging of the suffering and/or violence that we witnessed as children in our families. Our relationship to food is a microcosm of all that we learned about loving and being loved, about our self-worth. It is the stage upon which we reenact our childhood. If we were abused, we will abuse ourselves with food. The degree to which we are violent, abusive, self-punishing is in proportion to the degree of violence, abuse, and punishment we received. We learned how to do it by having it done to us.

❧✖❧

From a journal entry:

October 10, 1978.

Today I ate:

⅓ package graham crackers	100 calories
1 salad with dressing	300 calories
⅛ lb. carob chips	200 calories
1 cookie	75 calories
¼ lb. granola	300 calories
4 tbsp. cashew butter	300 calories
32 ounces apple juice	300 calories
½ Wayfarer's bread	250 calories
5 tbsp. hommus	300 calories
1 ice cream sandwich	400 calories
1 apple	76 calories
1 fudge bar	200 calories
1 package brown rice crackers	200 calories
1 tbsp. peanut butter	75 calories
½ gallon vanilla ice cream	2000 calories

DAY'S TOTAL CALORIES: 5176

October 11, 1978, 3 A.M.: I awaken with an image of myself slashing each organ in my body to pieces. With each strike I say, "Good. Again. Harder." I want to destroy myself. I want to eat until I die. The pain seems so deserving. It is the only way I am comfortable. Not slccping, eating uncontrollably, driving myself to the edge, this feels right. I want to get in my car and go to

Albertson's. 3 A.M. Bright lights. Eat ice cream. Be totally mad and fling myself into the ocean. Get rid of myself. I hate this creature that I am.

Good. Again. Harder.
I received this letter:

One thousand calories a day seemed like way too many to eat, so when I discovered that a calorie is really a kilocalorie, I multiplied everything I ate in a day by 100 and was disgusted by how much I was eating. I began eating smaller and smaller portions and finally got down to less than 100 calories a day. I ran five miles, I worked out with weights, I took two aerobic classes daily. I'm 5'9" and I weighed 100 pounds.

Good. Again. Harder.

Then I wanted to play soccer on the women's college team and the doctor told me I had to weigh 125 pounds, so I gained 50 pounds. Now I can't stop eating.

In the same letter, she says, "My mother left the five of us when we were babies. My dad died of alcoholism; the doctor said he had no liver left."

With no mother and an alcoholic father, there was no consistency, no solidity, no ground. With no mother and an alcoholic father, there was no one to receive her; it was not safe for her to express her feelings, so she didn't. She built a stage upon which to circumscribe and dramatize her feelings and the stage was called "My Problems with Food."

The obsession with food gives us a safe place into which we can place all our feelings of disappointment, rage, sorrow. As long as we are obsessed with food, we always have a concrete reason that explains our pain. Every hurt can be traced back, as one woman said, "to the Benedict Arnold in my life—food."

Most of us become so adept at denying or minimizing our pain that we believe our problems about food are only problems about food. We believe that our relationship to food and our bodies is the only area of our lives that we are in constant pain about, so once we have it solved, everything else will run smoothly.

I hear this in every single workshop. People believe this with such conviction, such utter dedication that when I say it isn't true, participants begin complaining about how uncomfortable the chairs are and how hot or cold it is in the room and they paid money to get here, why don't I have sweatshirts that fit them? Because if it is true that the pain in their lives is not about their weight, then what is it about?

For many of us, the only thing standing between us and years of caked-on, freeze-dried pain is our obsession with food. And rather than recognize that pain we throw ourselves into our obsession again and again, unconsciously believing that since food saved our life once, food will save it again.

⊗✕⊗

The last time I talked to my maternal grandmother was a week before she went into the hospital, two weeks before she died. It was the year I had gained fifty-five pounds, the year I was floundering, had quit school, was working as a maid and dishwasher. My grandmother said, "I think it's disgusting that you are not doing anything worthwhile; you're a good-for-nothing, a leech. For this, your dad sent you to college? To be a maid? I'm terribly disappointed in you and I'm sure I'm not the only one."

I wanted to say, "Go to hell" and slam the phone down. Instead, I got a lump in my throat and whispered, "I have to go now. Goodbye."

When she met my father for the first time, my grandmother

took my mother aside and said, "Most people have thirty-two teeth in their mouth, how come he has sixty-four?" When our family would spend spring vacation together, I would hear my grandmother talking about me through the peeling green plaster wall: "Don't you think she's gotten too fat, Ruthie? And she gets too much attention from her dad. He should pay more attention to Howard so that his daughter doesn't turn into a little snot."

When my mother was five, she came home one day to discover that her mother had shredded her favorite blanket and was using it for cleaning rags. What must it have been like to have my grandmother for a mother? Somewhere along the line, my mother stopped noticing and began walling herself off from her pain. Maybe it was when her mother taunted her about having to wear clothes from the Chubby Department of Macy's. Maybe it was when she was the first woman editor of her yearbook, brought home straight A's and no one noticed. Maybe it was when, in her first year of college, my grandmother said, "Your dad and I are moving to San Antonio. Either get married or come with us."

She walled herself off from her pain and built a stage on which to dramatize it instead. Drugs, alcohol, affairs, car accidents, illness, money, divorce. And always the obsession with food. In this way, the attention was on the pain of the drama instead of the pain that caused it.

❂✖❂

Beneath the passion for drama in a compulsive eater's life is the belief that without it we would not get what we want. Without drama we would simply be ourselves, and that is not good enough.

If I am myself and not Yvette Mimieux, no one will be interested in me.

If I am myself and not Lou Ann, Matt will not love me.

If I don't create a reason to be loved—being sick, being unhappy, being famous—if there is no urgency, no one will respond.

My everyday self is boring, chubby, clumsy. I say dumb things.

Each of these beliefs is preceded by an unspoken primary belief: "I *was* myself as a child and that didn't work. *If I had been a different self, I surely would have been loved.* Now I will try being someone else."

In many families, feelings were not discussed openly. Sadness, loneliness, fear, anger, appreciation, respect, tenderness were implied, talked around, or hidden. Often, we saw people most alive—their eyes lit, their bodies in motion—when they were frightened, angry at each other, or in a crisis. And if, when we were in a crisis, we received the attention we longed for, we learned that being our everyday selves did not soften the hearts of people around us. We needed something extra to awaken their love. A little excitement perhaps.

❃✖❃

A workshop participant describes her relationship with her father:

"I had three older brothers and my dad always wanted a girl, so when I came along I was the apple of his eye. When I went to the beach with him and sat on the edge of the water, I felt stronger than the ocean. He used to take me for rides in his truck every Saturday. He was a salesman, and when I got to go with him, I was very proud. But then business got bad and he started going away more and more, not even coming home on the weekends. When he was home, he yelled a lot. I once asked him what the word 'pedestrian' meant and he told me to stop being so nosy. But when I cried he would hold me, and when I was sick he would bring me presents. When I was about twelve or thirteen, I had the flu and stayed home from school. I ran up and down the stairs, putting hot towels on my head so that my temperature would go up and I would get sicker. I wanted to be real sick. I wanted my dad back."

When she talks about her present relationship with her husband, she says, "At the first sign of a cold, I feel relieved. When I broke my leg last year in a skiing accident, there was a part of me that was glad. I don't really believe I *create* illness, although I am sick a lot—with thyroid problems, migraines, and arthritis. But if Bill doesn't drop everything to be with me, I get angry, feel rejected. I want him to bring me tomato soup with saltine crackers and an ankle bracelet with my name on it."

If our reaction to events or feelings is "Oh good, this will get his/her attention," it is a sign that we believe we can't get what we want by being ourselves.

When I was in eleventh grade, *Vogue* magazine featured a model named Verushka, a windswept blond who looked remarkably like my mother. On the door of my locker, I pasted a photograph of Verushka in a slinky fuchsia gown with a feather boa around her neck. When friends asked about the photograph, I would say, "Why do you think I have it there?" Eventually, they gasped and said, "That's not your mother, is it?" And I smiled knowingly, a twinkle in my eye, as if to say, "Of course. Now will you think I'm special?"

☺✖☺

We create drama by lying, by suffering, by bingeing and dieting, by living in the midst of perpetual motion, by forever beginning or ending relationships. We create drama by externalizing our pain, by making things hard between ourselves in relationships instead of being honest about how hard it is *inside* ourselves. When we are not honest about the internal conflict, we stage an external one. We create drama because we are afraid of what would happen if we held still. We create drama because we are afraid of revealing ourselves. Creating drama protects us from being intimate.

Compulsive eating is fabulous theater. It is replete with all the elements of good tragedy: rage, frustration, grief, sorrow, fear, happiness, hope, exhilaration, ecstasy. Compulsive eating creates an illusion of excitement and participation. It simulates real life. You never have to do anything but go on extravagant binges and rigid diets, have four different-size wardrobes, and come closer and closer to your goal weight, while never actually reaching or maintaining it for longer than a week, to experience the vitality and intensity that most people define as being alive. You never have to do anything but absorb yourself in the cycle of losing and gaining weight to feel that you are involved in something exciting. You never have to let another human being come close.

Intimacy is showing another person the parts of ourselves that we believe to be unworthy and thereby risking that they will turn from us the way our parents did. (A voice inside screams: "It was excruciating the first time and now you're asking me to go through it again?") Intimacy brings with it tenderness and humor, companionship and affection, but it also demands that we relive the most agonizing moments of being a child.

We have the wrong idea about love. The songs we hear on the radio speak of passion and longing, but no one tells us they are describing the first—or last—six months of a relationship. When I speak to friends who are single, their main topic of conversation is of their sadness in living alone. They go to bed at night wishing they had a warm body to hold. Sunday magazine sections describe new and innovative companies that make love matches for their high-powered clients. Pay $3000 and you will have access to a library of video portraits among which is the promise of your perfect love. The Search for the Perfect Mate when you are single reminds me of The Dream to Be Thin when you are fat. The emphasis is on finding a mate or being thin, as if the act itself will ease the agony in our hearts. No one tells us that the hard part isn't finding a partner or losing weight; the hard part isn't *getting* there, it's being there. Which is the reason that we do all we can to prolong the process of getting there. We don't want to be there. We unconsciously decide that we would rather eat and be protected, or occupy our time with The Search, or find fault with our present relationship, than go back to the vulnerability of childhood that intimacy brings.

Matt and I can be taking a walk on the beach, laughing about the golden retriever that won't give the tattered blue Frisbee back to his owner when Matt will say something that triggers an old feeling, and by the time he looks at me again I am eight years old.

I didn't like being eight years old the first time; I don't want to go around again. So when feelings of eight-year-old helplessness and terror arise, I push them away. I tell myself they are ridiculous, selfish, childish. I withdraw, fold in on myself like a sea anenome. Matt senses the distance, asks me what is wrong. I say, "Nothing."

He says, "If nothing is wrong, then why are you looking at me as if you don't know me?" I tell him he is imagining things; he tells me I am not telling the truth. I tell him I don't like it when he accuses me of lying. In my desire to protect myself, I have created Drama #3567.

If I tell Matt the truth—that I suddenly feel like an eight-year-old, alone and scared that he isn't my friend any more—he might say, "You don't only feel like an eight-year-old, you act like one, too." He might say, "I can't stand how sensitive you are." He might laugh at me, yell at me, leave me. In my desire to avoid the hurt I felt as a child, I avoid the intimacy I lacked as a child.

In our present relationships, the possibility is that in speaking the truth, we'd go back in time to the moment when we learned not to speak the truth. Despite the love songs, despite the emphasis on finding a mate and being thin, the significance of either is in the process of reliving the agonizing moments of childhood, giving voice to the heretofore inexpressible, and becoming whole.

The significance of giving up the obsession with food is not a thinner body, not a smaller pants size, but giving up your protection from pain, for when you protect yourself from pain, you protect yourself from intimacy. When you allow your pain to be visible, you can give it a voice. And when you give it a voice, you can release yourself from it.

The significance of being intimate is not in finding a body to keep you warm at night or having a companion with whom to share your life; the significance is that in being close, you are thrown back to the time when you decided that being close was too scary, so you folded in on yourself. When you go back to that time, you give yourself the opportunity to be a child again, but this time with the power of an adult. You learn that you no longer have to hide your feelings to survive. And in so doing, you claim the precious parts of yourself—your trust, your faith, your honesty—that you locked away in a place where they would not be touched by the devastation in your family.

The problem with giving up drama—with food and in relationships—is that without it we don't know what to do. We're not sure we are really alive. We have to face something we never anticipated: the possibility of peace and contentment.

If we lived in family environments in which we felt that things were just about to fall apart, or always in the process of doing so, if we lived with emotional or physical violence, if we lived with abuse or neglect, then what is most familiar and therefore most comfortable to us is discomfort. We are suspicious of things that are easy or fluid or comfortable. Without theater, we feel as if we are missing the essentials of being alive. And in fact, we are. We are missing the drama that defined being alive in our families. We don't know how to be alive without it. To us, suffering dignifies an experience. When something is hard, we know it is worth doing. If we have to struggle, we have a purpose—and winning the struggle gives us a feeling of accomplishment.

There is no rest for a compulsive eater. We are either on our way up the scale or on our way down the scale. We are either lamenting what we look like today or wishing we looked the same as we did yesterday, when we were wishing we looked the same as we did last year. A woman in a workshop said, "I would die to be as thin as I was five years ago, when I would have died to be thinner." Contentment is unthinkable.

The same is true for intimacy. If we are comfortable with struggle and suffering, then we will choose partners who are not attracted to us, who are alcoholics or drug addicts, who are incapable of making a commitment. Or comfortable as we are with struggle and suffering, we will find a way to suffer in even the best relationships.

Peace and contentment are feelings that take practice to achieve. They are not a consequence of being successful or being in love or being thin. They are, among other things, a consequence of stopping in the present moment and looking around. For those of us who as children felt as if standing still meant being smashed, being content is perceived as a threat to our survival.

ᎭᎭᎭ

Last week I was opening the gate in our driveway, and as I was bending down to lock it in place, our neighbor Estelle was backing out of her driveway. She didn't see the open gate; her car crashed into the gate and the gate crashed into my head. Within a few minutes my forehead was hatching an egg under the skin. I stumbled back into the house for some ice and found the book *Naked Lunch* and six empty ice cube trays in the freezer. I made a mental note to torture Matt when I saw him again. Then I decided that I didn't have to act like a grown-up and then I began to sob, gulp, and wail. I envisioned myself getting a blood clot in my brain and being dead within forty-eight hours. I envisioned myself driving and suddenly becoming dizzy, losing control of the car and plunging into the ocean. I envisioned myself hitting Estelle with a baseball bat. I envisioned myself calling Matt at his meeting and telling him I had a concussion and could he come home immediately so that we could go to the hospital for a CAT scan. Instead, knowing that I was already late for my appointment with Maggie, my therapist, I got in the car and drove to her office.

I walked into her room decorated with the painting of a pink umbrella in a gauzy rain, and when she asked me how I was, I began to sob. I told her about Estelle and the frozen book and the blood clot and I showed her the egg on my head. She walked across the street to the King's Tavern for a bag of ice. I wrapped it in a towel and held it to my head. She told me it was highly unlikely I would get a blood clot in my brain, and instead of torturing him, why didn't I ask Matt why he put a book in the freezer instead of ice cubes. She told me it was unfortunate that I was standing at the gate when Estelle was backing out, but if I didn't feel nauseated or dizzy, the chances were good that all I had was a bump on the head.

"How unromantic," I said.

"Is a blood clot romantic?" she asked.

"Not exactly, but how about the fear of a blood clot? If everyone thought I might have a blood clot, they would appreciate me so much. Kind of like going to your own funeral and hearing every-one say how wonderful you are when you are still alive."

"You don't get to have both, Geneen. You either learn to change your internal dialogue to one of respecting yourself now, as regular and unromantic as you sometimes are, or you live in great swoops of emotion, always afraid that the moment the dust settles, people will see the 'real' you and reject you."

Silence.

"Is a blood clot romantic?" she asked again.

And I thought of green hair, epilepsy, discarded Baby Ruth bars. Lou Ann.

"Only if being alive isn't," I answered.

CHAPTER
4

Wanting What
Is Forbidden

As part of my meditation practice, I participate in silent retreats at which no talking, no eye contact, no touching is allowed. During the first one I attended, I fell madly in love with a man across the room. By the end of the retreat, I was certain that I would marry him. For those who question the feasibility of falling in love with someone you've never exchanged looks or words with, here's a description of courting in silence:

Day #1:

I arrive at the Metaphysics Institute in the California desert, suddenly feeling out of place and wondering why I came. They assign me to a room with a woman named Rosalyn who wears cobalt-blue Spandex pants and a pink-and-yellow flowered blouse. She pops her bubble gum as she unpacks her clothes.

I see the schedule for the first time posted outside the dining room: Fifteen hours of walking or sitting meditation, not speaking to anyone, not looking at anyone . . . for TEN DAYS. I break my vow of silence immediately and ask the woman next to me if this is a joke. I decide that Alexandra, who told me about the retreat but didn't mention the schedule, is no longer my friend. Is my enemy. Forever.

Day #2

I go to the sittings. I have a matching cushion and meditation mat—rose with a gray center. After the first forty-five-minute session, my back hurts. My knee aches. The lady in front of me snores. I want to throw rocks at the teacher, whose voice is saccharine.

Day #3

I want to leave. Keep on falling asleep during meditation. Eight more days of this—my God. I want it to be over. I always want things to be over. I live with one foot out the door—at movies, plays, relationships. This really isn't any different from that. Where am I going when I leave? It's not as if things are so much better when I arrive from wherever it is that I can't wait to leave.

Day #5

It drags interminably. My mood is vacant but irritable. I looked forward to the five o'clock snack of sunflower seeds and fruit as if it were going to save me, but then it wasn't what I wanted. Actually what I wanted was to feel better and food didn't do it. ("You get to see that you are no happier after you eat than before," one of the teachers said last night.)

Day #6

There is a very attractive man here. He has curly black hair, horn-rimmed glasses, tailored clothes. The Man from *Esquire*. What should I call him? Robert? No, I've always wanted a Michael as a lover . . . and so Michael it is. Our eyes almost met yesterday; "Hmm," I thought, "you're lovely."

I know what shoes he wears, where he sits in the meditation

hall. A few more days and I'll know what he puts in his coffee. A major drawback in our budding romance is that we can't speak to each other. In my fantasy, he drives me to the airport; we begin to like each other a lot. I see him again and again. Oh, how lovely to be in love.

Day #7

The teacher says, "Give a name to a sensation in your body."
Longing.
The teacher says, "Where is it?"
In my chest.
The teacher says, "What color is it?"
Blue.
The teacher says, "Be specific."
Blue twisted rope of longing to the right side of my heart.
The teacher says, "What is it about?"
Longing for rest. Longing for completion. Longing for satisfaction.
Longing for someone to walk into my chest and make me whole.
I never long for what I already have.
If I only love what I long for, have I confused longing with loving?

Day #8

My mind wanders to fantasies like a beggar to food. It keeps yanking me out of the present. At snack time, I was fantasizing about going to Mexico with Michael. By the time I had finished the snack of carob chips and raisins, I was running with him on the black sand beach, making love with him under the ceiling fan in the thatched-roof palapa.

Day #9

During the walking meditation today, as I was supposed to be "lifting-moving-placing," "lifting-moving-placing" first one foot and then the other, as I was supposed to be heightening my awareness of the sensations of the back of my foot as it touched the pavement, supposed to be noticing each muscle it took to move that leg, during the afternoon meditation as I was supposed to be expanding my mindfulness and moving closer to the detachment of desire and the five hindrances, as I was supposed to be inching my way toward enlightenment and the elimination of suffering for all sentient beings, I was intently focused on the muscles it took for Michael to move his right buttock in his faded blue jeans. My powerful awareness was focused on the movement of Michael's ass as he lifted, moved, and placed first one leg and then the other on the stairs of the main hall. I was heightening my awareness by imagining the sensations of his slender dark-haired fingers on my face, his-heart shaped lips on my neck. I was noticing the throbbing in my chest as I imagined him whispering that he loved me. I was moving toward the universal oneness by attuning my body so closely to his that when he took a step, my calf muscles were inspired to move. The pinnacle of my journey to enlightenment took place at the evening walking meditation when I walked alongside Michael to the set of stairs and noticed that he was closing his eyes, keeping his hand on the railing as he lifted, moved, and placed first one foot and then the other on his way down the steps. With great mindfulness, I moved to the opposite side of the railing, closed my eyes, balanced myself with my hand, and began lifting, moving, placing my feet up the stairs. And then it happened: a sudden jolt of warmth, matter meeting matter, Michael's elegant hand contacting mine. I opened my eyes. He opened his. The corners of his mouth turned up in a smile, his teeth shone in the violet evening. Then he quickly averted his eyes and continued his long passage to liberation.

Day #10

The retreat is over. We broke silence today in a large circle; we each spoke our name and two sentences about ourselves. Michael's real name is Ralph Sheen. He just spent six months on a meditation retreat and is leaving for China in four months, but until then he will be living in Santa Cruz. Of all the places in the country, he will be living in the same city that I do. This relationship is meant to be.

Ralph and me at the beach when the sunset spills glittering washes of gold and turquoise on the sand; Ralph and me in my brass-and-iron bed with the french windows open to the plum blossoms on the deck; Ralph and me holding hands, making love, getting married in a midnight ceremony next to a lake with ten thousand candles floating on the water.

But first I must introduce myself to him.

❀✗❀

Ralph wasn't married, didn't have a woman in his life, wasn't an alcoholic or a workaholic, and didn't take drugs. Ralph had dimples and doe eyes. He covered his mouth when he laughed. He raised his pinkie when he drank from a glass. He said he wanted to find "an intense woman" who could show him parts of himself he tried to avoid. Ralph was completely and utterly available. The only problem was that he said he was not attracted to me. If you can call that a problem. I certainly didn't. I believed that Ralph didn't know what he wanted and it was my job to convince him that he wanted *me*.

I liked Ralph's face. I liked his walk. I liked his hands. I liked the way his hair curled over his collar. I liked his voice and his laugh. So much that I wanted to spend my life with him, and I was not going to let anything or anyone get in my way. Especially Ralph.

On our way to a postretreat picnic in Nisene Marks Park, we stopped at Gayle's Bakery and laughed as we chose four desserts for the two of us: a cream puff, marzipan cake, chocolate mousse, and praline cheesecake.

He's having a good time with me. Surely he is attracted to me. You don't giggle like this with someone you are not attracted to.

After our main course of cheese sandwiches and potato salad, I pulled out the desserts. First the cream puff, he said, as he licked the cream from the edge of the pastry. There's a little cream left on your lips, I said, here let me fix that—and I kissed him. He kissed me back. We kissed each other's necks, lips, hands, eyes . . .

He likes me, see? He likes me, you don't kiss someone you don't like, you don't kiss someone you are not attracted to, he's getting aroused. I knew it, I knew it.

After we made love, Ralph said, "This doesn't mean anything. I still don't know whether I'm attracted to you. I got carried away and it was nice, but it doesn't mean anything."

"Uh-huh," I nodded. "I know."

Sure, Ralph, sure. I know you are afraid of really loving someone, I don't know why, maybe you have been hurt, but whatever it is, I understand and I will be patient because I know you will come to love me.

Ralph told me three times in six weeks that he didn't want to be lovers. He also told me that he loved me. He said, "If you hang in here with me, I know I can learn. I have a hard time with intimacy." He made love with me the day before he left for China. "Let me in," he asked, "please let me in." He didn't have to ask.

During the eleven months he was away, Ralph sent me three

postcards and one letter. I sent him a thirty-eight-page letter that I kept over a period of three months instead of a journal. I told him about my walks on the beach, I told him about the sunsets, about the medjool dates I saw in the market. In my chirpiest voice, I described every detail of my life except the fact that I was saving myself for him, soaking myself in the fantasy of our life together.

I didn't miss physical affection, I didn't miss sharing my life with anyone, I didn't even miss Ralph. I didn't know him well enough to miss him. I had what I needed to make me happy, I had what was most familiar to me: the illusion of love.

❧✖❧

During his absence, I moved into a house by the ocean that I lovingly decorated with him in mind. Heart-shaped wreaths, beige lace curtains, candles on the window ledge. Quilts, baskets, flowers. This will be our home, I will live here with him, we will be happy in this blue wooden house by the sea.

In the two years I was in love with him, I saw Ralph a total of twenty-two days. He traveled around the world, he went to meditation retreats, he lived with friends in Berkeley. He told me he was *not* attracted to me, he told me he didn't *know* whether he was attracted to me, he told me he *was* attracted to me. When I saw him, I never knew if he would greet me as a friend, a lover, or a stranger. He told me that I did not fit his picture of an ideal woman. When he pointed to a woman whom he considered attractive, I found myself looking at an eighty-five-pound wisp with bleached blond hair.

Sara wanted to storm Ralph's apartment in the middle of the night and drop bowling balls on his head. She wanted to stick straight pins in his eyes. She wanted to maim and strangle him. She wanted me to stop maiming myself. She pleaded, she yelled: "You have to get out of this relationship before you lose every shred of sanity you have. First he tells you he's not attracted to you, then he sleeps with you, then he tells you to hang in there with him, then he tells you he *is* attracted to you, then he leaves for a year . . . He's s-i-c-k, Ralph is a *sick* little boy who thinks there is a perfect woman waiting for him somewhere, which is a sure sign that he doesn't want to be in a relationship. He isn't interested in finding out why he's so crazy, he doesn't care what his craziness does to you, he doesn't think about your feelings at all. You deserve so much more, Geneen, a partner who sees how special you are, not this sicko. Call him and tell him you never want to see him again. I'll dial the number, I'll stand next to you when you say it. Do it today, *now*."

I couldn't. I wouldn't. I felt as if Ralph was my only chance for happiness and that if I let him go, I would be filled with the despair of nightmare monsters with hollow eyes and empty hands. I had to have him, and that was that. No one could convince me that I was wrong. I forgave him his absence, his negligence, his utter lack of kindness. He didn't ask me to forgive him, but I did. I believed that I needed him to be fully alive. It was as if someone turned up the dial marked "vibrance" when he walked in the room; what was dull without him became miraculous with him. Color, sound, taste. Flowers, birds, ice cream. The place in me that knew laughter and beauty had his name on it. With Ralph, anything was possible. With Ralph, I was safe. When I wasn't with Ralph, I was alone, no matter who I was with.

I wouldn't answer Sara when she would yell, "If *this* is safe, what is unsafe?" I had to protect myself, protect Ralph from her recriminations. I wouldn't let myself think about why he would let weeks pass without calling me, why he wouldn't tell his friends about me.

I hung on to moments with him, golden moments. Ralph and me at Adelita's on my birthday, eating tortillas and enchiladas, holding hands. Ralph saying, "You are everything I want." Ralph and me on my bed in the red heat of summer, looking at a book of paintings by Georgia O'Keeffe; he turns to me and says, "You are such a joy to be with." Cameo moments.

At the end of our second year "together," Ralph was accepted into a gourmet cooking school in Berkeley. We were sitting in the back yard when he told me that he was moving. "I'll be going to Berkeley," he said, "and I am not planning on visiting you, nor does it make much difference to me whether you visit me."

I stared at him, uncomprehending. He's not really saying this. He doesn't really mean this. He has to be kidding. Two years of living my life around this man and he's telling me it doesn't make a difference to him whether we see each other any more?

"Tell me again. Tell me what you just said," I told him.

He repeated it: "I'm moving to Berkeley and I don't think we should plan on seeing each other."

"You schmuck—get out of my house."

Ralph looked mildly surprised. "I still want to be your friend," he said. "That's what I have always been interested in. But I just don't think we should make tremendous efforts in that direction. I mean, if it happens that we run into each other, I'd always be interested in hearing about your life and what's going on."

"Get out." My face was flushed, my voice was shaking. I walked past the heart-shaped wreath to the front door, opened it, and turned to face him. He smiled. I blinked.

And then he left.

❀✖❀

It was not strength that enabled me to tell Ralph to leave; it was not because I didn't want him or love him, and it was certainly not because I believed that I deserved better. There was simply no way I could fit his sentence and the sentiment it expressed into the fantasy I had been drenched in for two years.

In my fantasy, Ralph needed time. I had given him years. In my fantasy, Ralph loved me but needed to explore his fears of intimacy. I had encouraged him to start therapy, and after some resistance, he had found a therapist he liked. In my fantasy, therapy would help him realize that although he might have issues of control or abandonment, there was a woman—me—who because of her perceptiveness and patience, understood him and had been waiting faithfully for him to appreciate her as his ideal.

In my fantasy, the man who didn't care that his leaving caused such despair in the girl-child he left would finally care. And he would stay. Stay, stay, he would finally stay.

I told Ralph to leave because I recognized that he already had.

☹✖☺

I knew my involvement with Ralph represented an unconscious and very powerful struggle, but I had no idea what it was and I felt helpless to stop it. During those two years, I felt as if I were a puppet, obeying commands that were familiar but no longer authentic. My words seemed contrived, my actions seemed wooden, and yet I flung myself into the role with a ferocious abandon, as if being with Ralph were literally a matter of living or dying. As if I were a child and he were the adult I depended upon for my survival.

Children must deny and ignore what causes them pain. Children must cling lovingly to those who abuse them, because given the choice between an abusive person and no one at all, there is no choice. The difference between someone and no one is the difference between life and death. Children must be ever-faithful, patient, responsive, forgiving, and willing to take horrendous abuse without saying no. Children must build elaborate fantasies that turn the people who abuse and leave them to people who love and adore them. Because of their ability to fantasize—and to actually believe that what they are fantasizing is or will someday be true—children can endure their suffering.

If a parent is absent, unavailable, abusive, or dead, it is extraordinarily useful and often necessary to create a fantasy world in which that parent or a parent figure is alive, available, and loving. The exact nature of the fantasy will depend on the reasons fantasy is necessary: If a father is violent, he may be imbued with tenderness; if a mother is often absent, she will become readily available. The fantasy is created in counterpoint to the pain of everyday life. All that is flawed becomes sublime. Excuses are made for inexcusable behavior: my mom didn't mean to hit me, she is just tired; my dad loves me so much that he works hard to buy me pretty things and that is why he is not here.

❧✖❧

My friend Melissa's parents were divorced when she was ten. On a sultry night in August, her father drove away from the house in his pickup truck without telling her goodbye. She didn't talk to him again until she was twenty-five. For three years after the divorce and her family's move to Wyoming, her mother told her that they would be going back to California any day. Melissa kept her suitcase packed under her bed; she missed her daddy. Forgetting that he had been gone for eight to ten months every year and that when he was home, he was fighting with her mother, reading the newspaper, watching baseball, basketball, or football on television and drinking beer, she crowned her daddy king of her heart. Her mother yelled and punished and cried, but her daddy was kind, her daddy was generous, her daddy would save her from the misery of living in Wyoming. Her daddy who disappeared for fifteen years. Her perfect daddy.

The agony of a child whose father left without saying goodbye is unbearable. Her mother would not tolerate Melissa's feelings; she was not allowed to even mention her father's name. Without an adult to comfort her and validate her right to feel sad and lonely and angry, Melissa needed to transform her anguish into feelings she could live with. So she created a fantasy world in which her father wanted her as much as she wanted her father, but because of his job, and lack of finances, he could not write, call, or visit. But if he did, oh if he did, life would be glorious. They would go surfing, eat Cheerios, never have to make the bed.

When we are children, our parents have cloudless eyes and creamy skin. They are big and strong, they know everything, they are perfect. Parents strengthen this perception by teaching us that they are always right and that children should be seen and not heard. We learn to listen and obey. No one teaches us that parents are selfish. No one teaches us that parents lie. No one teaches us that they need us to complete them as much as we need them to love us. We could not get angry at our parents; we were not allowed. Instead, when they got drunk and blamed us for their behavior, told us it was because we did not do the dishes, we believed them. When they hit us with brooms and sticks and told us they were doing it for own good, we believed them. When they crept into our bedrooms late at night and put their hands under our pajamas, touched us in private places and told us we asked for it, we believed them. We told ourselves that if only we were prettier, didn't have so many pimples, had straight blond hair instead of frizzy brown hair, if only we shared our toys, didn't cry so much, said please and thank you, if only we weren't who we were, our mothers would be sober and our fathers wouldn't leave for fifteen years. *If only we were thin.*

Those of us who are compulsive eaters believe *with a vengeance* that if we were thin, our lives would be drastically different. Even those people who have lost weight and been thin six or seven times in their lives persist in believing that when they get thin again, one more time—just give us one more chance, this time you'll see—they will once and for all be happy.

The When I Am Thin fantasy has been invaluable to us throughout our lives. We constructed it to explain our childhood despair and prevent it from destroying us. We needed something, someone upon whom to place the responsibility for the pain.

The problem with letting go of the fantasy now is that without it, nothing stands between us and the despair of a lifetime. As compulsive eaters, we have spent years telling ourselves that we are not lovable because we are not thin, that when we do get thin, the people we want will want us, our love will be returned tenfold, our agony will disappear. We will be vindicated for all those loveless years. That fantasy was our bulwark against our pain; it excused our parents, while giving us hope that at a given moment in time—when we lost weight—our lives would be silky and tender as water lilies. But it was only a child's way of making sense. Our weight had nothing to do with the reasons our parents abused or left or violated us. We had nothing to do with the reasons our parents abused or left or violated us. We believed we did because blaming ourselves for the sorrow gave us some measure of control over it.

During the years I spent dieting, I believed that every single trouble in my life was rooted in my weight. When I walked into a store and they didn't have my size, when I walked into a gathering of people and no one paid attention to me, when I couldn't decide on work I wanted to do and felt lazy and useless and stupid, when I found myself alone every Saturday night, I believed that my unhappiness had to do with my body. I believed that as long as I stayed fat, I was stifling my creativity, my self-expression, my beauty. When I allow myself to be thin, I told myself, it will be symbolic of my willingness to receive pleasure; being thin will be my statement to myself and the world that after so many years, I finally believe I am worthy of love.

I was wrong. Being thin did what being thin can do: it helped me feel lighter and more attractive on a daily level and by society's standards. It did not heal the underlying suffering and repressed anguish of childhood. And it never will.

❧✖❧

Married men, long-distance relationships, lovers who are addicted to drugs or work or alcohol or sex—pursuing them is the same as believing that when you get thin, the anguish that follows you like a shadow will disappear. Both are fantasies; one involves achieving something; the other involves getting someone. Both are a way of saying, "The present (or past) might be awful, but I don't have to think about it because the future will be glorious." Both are designed to distract you; they both provide a focus, a goal that you can constantly move toward without ever arriving.

❧✖❧

Melissa is now forty-four years old. She has a husband, a daughter, work, money, a house in the mountains, and a married lover. Her lover, like her father, is always threatening to leave. Her lover, like her father, is someone she longs for, desires to spend her life with, believes will save her from the misery of daily life. She is convinced that if she were married to her lover and not her husband, she would be sexually fulfilled, completely understood and appreciated for the complex woman she is, just as she was convinced that living with her father would be a glorious adventure—a life without tears, punishment, or chores.

Melissa says she wants to live with her lover. Her lover says he doesn't know what he wants. Sometimes he tells her that he is going to leave his wife; sometimes he tells her that they must forget about each other; sometimes he tells her that he cannot live without her. Melissa waits. Melissa knows how to wait. She spent fifteen years waiting to speak to her perfect daddy again.

If Melissa stopped waiting for love to come home, she might start wondering why it is taking so long. She might even get angry at the heartlessness of a man who disappeared from his daughter's life without even a phone call for fifteen years . . . and then showed up pretending that nothing had happened. If she stopped waiting, she might start weeping. She might feel betrayed, abandoned, hopeless. She might, for the first time since her father left, feel the betrayal she locked away and will never acknowledge as long as she believes that a bright and loving future will be hers if she can wait long enough.

Recently, Melissa has been getting sick with flus, skin infections, sprained ankles. She is concerned that her body is breaking down. She says she is falling apart. I say, "If your body were trying to talk to you, what would it say?" She says, "I have to stop living the way I am living. I keep waiting for Marcus [her lover] to make up his mind, but I don't even know what I want to do. After three and a half years of sneaking around, it's really beginning to get to me."

She has been sneaking around for longer than three and a half years. Sneaking around her mother, sneaking around her husband, sneaking around herself. She cannot tell the truth anywhere, to anyone. After a lifetime of silencing the feelings that could threaten the people around her, she now no longer knows what she feels—only what she thinks she is allowed to feel. After thirty-four years of hiding herself so well, Melissa is left rattling with emptiness and disturbed by the sensation that the life she is living is not her own.

❀✖❀

My friend Clara told me a story about a client of hers, an eight-year-old child who had been on a diet for two years and had gained fourteen pounds in the process. In desperation, her mother consulted Clara; Clara asked what her daughter's favorite food was. "M&Ms," the mother replied.

"Good. I want you to leave here and buy enough M&Ms to

fill a pillowcase. After you've done that, give the filled pillowcase to your daughter and let her eat the candy whenever she wants. As soon as the supply is diminished, refill it. Make sure she always has a full pillowcase of M&Ms. Take her off the diet, let her eat whatever she wants when she is hungry, and call me in a week."

After shrieking with horror and telling Clara that if her daughter gained fifty pounds, she was going to send her to live at Clara's house, the mother crept out of Clara's office, into a supermarket, and then home to her linen closet.

Her daughter carried the pillowcase of M&Ms around with her for eight days. She slept with it, she set it beside the tub when she took a bath, she put it in a chair when she watched television. And, of course, she helped herself to M&Ms whenever she wanted them. Which, the first few days, was very often. In fact, after her mother bought three more pounds of M&Ms on the third day of this sugar-coated experience, she was ready to sue Clara. In a hysterical phone call, she told her that her child was eating more candy than ever before and how the hell was she supposed to lose weight doing *this*? Clara reassured her that her daughter was reacting to the years of deprivation and that when she believed, really believed, that she could eat whatever she wanted and that her mother was not waiting to snatch her pillowcase away, she would relax and begin eating from stomach hunger.

On the ninth day, the pillowcase stayed in the bedroom. By the end of five weeks, her daughter had forgotten the M&Ms and had lost six pounds.

❀✖❀

The fantasy of the taste of M&Ms is more enchanting than the taste of M&Ms. The fantasy of being thin is more powerful than being thin. The fantasy of spending your life with a partner who

is unavailable is more exciting than spending your life with someone who does not love you.

As children from troubled families, we spent our lives wanting
what was forbidden to us: love. And because we never received
it, we still believe it is forbidden. We bargain with an unseen
authority: if we eat only diet wafers and protein drinks, if we
torture and deprive ourselves enough, whittle our bodies down
to their bare bones, *then* will we be the lovable children our
parents didn't notice?

We act as if we were those children—conniving, waiting,
demeaning ourselves for love. We are not attracted to people who
are tender with us; rather we attract relationships that repeat the
wounds of the past.

A workshop participant said she could describe her history of
relationships by saying that she spent fifty years trying to make
the wrong people stay.

When they do stay, when a married man leaves his wife for
his mistress, when a long-distance relationship becomes a live-
in partnership, the fantasy is shattered. The lovers we were willing
to die for become ordinary human beings who crunch their cereal
too loud and fart in their sleep. It is not the Ralphs and the
workaholics and the married men we want: we want the love we
didn't get from our mothers and fathers.

☺✕☺

After a year of making scenes at airports when Matt went on a
trip, I realized it wasn't him that I wanted to stay; I wanted my
father to stay and protect me from my mother. I needed him,
and when he left I felt terrified and deserted. If Matt stayed in
the house for the next sixty years, if he never went to the grocery
store or for a walk around the block, I still would not be able to
change the fact that I felt terrified and deserted when my father
left. When I stopped trying to make the wrong person stay, and

began allowing myself to feel the pain and anger at the person I wanted to stay—pain I spent thirty-five years trying to avoid—I stopped making scenes at airports.

❸✖❸

Fantasy and wanting what is forbidden are about our desire to shut out the pain of our past. It was valuable to make gods and goddesses out of people we needed as children. Longing for what we could not have gave us hope that one day we would receive it and our lives would be better. Fantasy and longing were our friends.

The problem with fantasy is the greatest benefit of fantasy: it prevents us from living in the present moment. But the present now is different from the present then, and while it is true that in the present, people still get sick, leave, and die, it is also true that the present is where hearts are opened and love enters.

CHAPTER
5

The One-Wrong-Move Syndrome

Matt and I returned from a trip and had a fight. My suitcases were open in my study and clothes, books, papers were strewn everywhere. In the kitchen, filled with muddy water, was a pot I had scorched the night before we left. The mosaic of unfinished tasks and half-made decisions I had left behind seemed overwhelming. Within thirty minutes of being home, I wanted to crawl out of my life.

Matt, on the other hand, was radiant. When I walked into his office, his suitcases were open, too, his clothes, books, and papers littered every inch of space, but he was leaning back in his gray leather chair, feet resting on the shirts that were tumbled on his desk, laughing, as he talked on the phone. Blanche, our cross-eyed seventeen-pound male cat, was purring on his lap.

"Thanks," Matt was saying. "It feels great to be back. And it's always good to hear that I was missed." He gave me a look that said: Do you want to talk to me? I nodded. He mouthed the words "A few minutes." I said, "Fine."

But it wasn't fine. As I closed the door to his room, I decided that I was living with an insensitive jerk who denies his feelings. And if there's anything I can't stand, I muttered to myself, it's someone who says he's happy in the midst of grievous circumstances. It makes me feel crazy. It makes me feel as if I'm back in my family, telling my father that there is something wrong and he is laughing as he says, no sweetheart, no honey, no pussycat, nothing is wrong, everything is fine between your mother and me. By the time Matt got off the phone, I had worked myself into a frenzy.

"I can't believe you're sitting in there, feet up on the desk tra-la, as if there's nothing to do around here. How about the mail, the garden, the glass we forgot to recycle, the pot in the sink? Everywhere there is something to do and you're just in your office with the door closed, laughing in your own little world as if it's Mardi Gras."

The corners of Matt's eyes began to crinkle. I knew that a half-smile would cross his face next. My mother used to tell me to wipe that smile off my face or she'd send me flying into the middle of next week.

"What's so funny?" I asked. "I *hate* it when you laugh at me."

"How old are you right now?" he asked.

That question was supposed to be my signal, according to a prearranged agreement, that I had been triggered by something in the moment that brought me back into a painful childhood place.

I wasn't buying it. This time, I decided, I was right and he was wrong and anyone with a foot in the door of reality would agree.

"What a dumb question. How old do you think I am?" I retorted.

"Punky," he said softly, "have you forgotten that I am your friend, not your enemy? If you're feeling overwhelmed, you can just say that. Tell me you need help. Tell me what I can do. You don't have to push me away."

"You are *not* my friend." (I am six years old; it is summer. Nancy and I are sitting on the stoop of the house on Eightieth Street, having just finished a game of potsie. Nancy has naturally curly hair that falls in jet black ringlets around her face and onto her sleeveless candy-striped shirt. She is saying, "My birthday is

in April and yours is in August. I'm older than you and I knew
your mother before you did." I feel as if she's just punched me
in the stomach. It's not fair, she's *my* mother, how come she
didn't tell me she knew Nancy before she knew me? I stare at
Nancy. I wish I was her. I wish I had her curly hair. I wish I
had known my mother first. I think hard about how to get back
at her. Finally I say, "Okay, smarty pants, you might have known
my mother before I did, but since you were born before me,
you're going to die before me, too."

"I am not," she says.

"Are too."

"Am not."

"Are too."

"Am not."

"You're not my friend any more," I say, putting an end to the
conversation immediately.)

"I'm not your friend?" Matt is asking incredulously. "You make
life so hard on yourself. Even now when you have someone who
wants to love you more than anyone has ever loved you, you
insist on toughing it out alone."

I open my mouth to say that a friend of mine would not sit
in his office laughing while I am out here with burnt pots and
growing mail, but I am losing ground; the words sound frayed at
the corners. Instead I say, "I don't know how to reach out when
I feel like I'm alone. I push you away because I believe you have
already gone away and I don't want to seem like an idiot reaching
out to someone who doesn't love me. If I felt I could—if, in that
moment, I believed that you cared about me and wanted to
help—I wouldn't push you away."

"You knew I loved you an hour ago. Suddenly you think I
don't?"

I nod my head yes, the tears caught in my throat. If I speak
now, I know the words will come out in the same high-pitched
accusatory tone in which I have heard Sasha, who is three years

old, say to Sara, with tears gushing down her face, "You bit the head off the buffalo animal cookie and now she can't see."

At the same time, I feel bewildered and alone and I don't want to pretend that I am fine. As soon as Matt repeats what he hears me saying, it *sounds* ridiculous but *feels* like the truth.

Being able to move from apparent confidence to utter desolation in the time it takes a star to fall is one of the symptoms of being in an adult body and experiencing life through the shattered eggshell of childhood.

It seemed to me as a child that in one moment everything was fine and in the next moment, everything had fallen apart. On Tuesday I could say to my mom, "Will you help me with my homework tonight?" and she would say, "Of course, darling." On Wednesday, I could say, "Will you help me with my homework tonight?" and she would say, "Why can't you do it yourself? Why are you always asking me for something? Can't you see I am busy? Don't you think about anyone but yourself?" Sometimes she slapped me across the face. I spent hours in my room going over and over what I had done and wondering why I always thought about myself first and why I didn't consider her; I hated myself. One night I tried pulling all my hair out. I was dumb and fat and selfish and I wanted to hurt myself.

❧✖❧

Julia, a woman in a workshop, tells a story about her father leaving when she was five and her mother's taking her to Miami to begin a new life. A life in which divorce was unheard of and in which being a single mother was not attractive or socially accepted. So her mother lied to her friends and said she moved to Miami alone and didn't have any children. Julia was not allowed to answer the phone, not allowed to go out in public with her mother. When she forgot to obey rules, she was punished severely, sent to her room without dinner or kisses or bedtime stories. Julia grew up believing that if she made one wrong move, said the wrong thing, acted in a way that was not pleasing to her teacher or friend or lover, she would be punished. After fifty years, she is still trying hard to be perfect. She doesn't want to go to bed without kisses.

❃✖❃

The one-wrong-move syndrome is not something you do; it's a way that you are. Your words and actions are tinged with the urgent knowledge that your future rests on doing the right thing in this moment, now. If you make a mistake, you will ruin everything. The world is divided into good and bad, right and wrong, black and white. There are no grays, no in-betweens; there is no room for paradox; there is no past, there is no mercy. If you ask about homework on the wrong night, if you pick up the phone when you are not supposed to, you will not be forgiven. If you are not perfect, you are bad. And if you are bad, you are terrible. The judgments are relentless.

When you grow up believing that you are loved because of what you do, not who you are, your survival depends on doing the right thing. If you make one wrong move you believe you will die.

The one-wrong-move syndrome is a description of a reaction to a feeling, event, or person in which it seems that in one moment everything is fine and in the next moment there is nothing, not one single thing that is right or good in your world. The one-wrong-move syndrome is a description of what it feels like to be a reasonably confident adult one moment and a terrified child the next.

❃✖❃

You wake up in the morning confident that today will be a two-pounds-thinner day, even better than yesterday, when you lost

1¼ *pounds; you put on your in-between pants, not the smallest size that's hanging in your closet but not the largest size either. You notice that they zip easily with a thumb's worth of room to spare, which is very different from two weeks ago when you had to pour yourself into them and hold your stomach in all day, breathing in short shallow spurts to keep the button from popping and your awareness from the uncomfortable sensation of being squeezed to death. You eat your poached egg on dry toast for breakfast, your apple for your mid-morning snack. For lunch, you eat a piece of cold broiled chicken without the skin and three slices of tomato, all the while congratulating yourself on how good you are being, how much weight you will lose. You reward yourself for the deprivation you feel by the vision of the thin you entering a room. All heads turn as unsuspecting people are practically knocked off their chairs, so startled are they by the magnificence of your smile, your eyes, your lithe body. Today would be a good day to go shopping, you tell yourself, try on a few clothes, see how good you look in smaller sizes. So you get in the car and begin driving to your favorite store, but as you come to a stoplight, you realize that something is wrong. Something is gnawing at you. You can't put it into words, but as you sit there, it grows more and more oppressive until you feel you'll suffocate under the weight of it. You're having a hard time breathing, the anxiety is rising and you want it to stop. All you care about is having it stop, and you begin thinking about the eclairs in the bakery next to the clothes store. Suddenly you are relieved. Something will take this feeling away. You don't have to come apart. You will not suffocate. With the determination of a samurai, you steer the car to the parking lot, click click click go your shoes on the pavement. You look at the man with tortoiseshell glasses who is passing on your left but you don't really see him, you don't see anything, your mind is a laser beam of intent. You want the food. Then you are standing in front of the glass case, hearing yourself order not one but four eclairs, five cookies, and a marzipan cake. You mutter something about having a party as you pay for your relief and leave. Click click click on the pavement, the sound of car door opening, the thud of its slamming shut and finally, finally, you are alone with your blessed relief. Quickly, frantically, and without tasting them, you inhale two eclairs. At a more leisurely pace, you eat a third. Your stomach is getting full; you can feel the whipped cream sloshing against your ribs, can feel your pants getting tighter. Oh shit. You've blown it. You've fucking blown it. You were doing so well, sixteen days of eating dry toast and skinless chicken and you blew it in one afternoon. Ten minutes. Ten lousy minutes and sixteen days are ruined. Ten lousy minutes and your whole life is ruined. One wrong move. Why did you have to go to the bakery? Why couldn't you just have walked into the clothes store? Why can't you do anything right? You knew it really wasn't any use trying to lose weight, you knew it all the time, you shouldn't have even tried. You can feel your skin stretching right now, this second, your stomach is getting bigger, it's no use trying to get your weight under control, you might as well give up. Just the way you give up on everything.*

⚙✖⚙

We eat the way we live. What we do with food, we do in our lives. Eating is a stage upon which we act out our beliefs about ourselves. As compulsive eaters, we use food to somatize our deepest fears, dreams, and convictions. Something is wrong when we find ourselves reeling into paroxysms of despair from eating a piece of garlic bread or three eclairs. Something is wrong when we feel we have to deprive ourselves of foods we love because we believe we would abuse them—or ourselves—if we allowed them in our lives. Something is wrong and we are using food to express it.

❀✖❀

I remember the feeling of creeping around the house when I suspected my mother was in a bad mood. I would tiptoe on the carpet, open and close doors with painstaking slowness so that she wouldn't hear me. Most of the time, I would sit on the orange flowered carpet in my bedroom and not move. Not rustle English papers, not go to the bathroom, not open or shut any drawers. I was walking a fine line between safety and madness and I knew it. One wrong move and my mother would go into a rage• of purple hysteria. One wrong move and all I would know was the clap of flesh hitting flesh, red fingernails scratching my arms, the pain in my head of being pulled across the room by my hair. One wrong move and all I would care about was living through the one wrong move I had made.

A workshop participant named Rita describes her life as a seven-year-old: "My mother died when I was six. My dad married the maid. They were both alcoholics. By the time I was seven, I knew the phone number of every bar in town. When it got to be ten or eleven clock at night, I walked to the bar and fetched my dad. He got very mad at me for interrupting him with his buddies, and sometimes he hit me right there, but usually he waited till we got home. I climbed into the driver's seat of his car and drove us home. When my stepmother was involved, she hit me worse than my dad. One time she broke my arm."

A woman friend talks about being thrown in the closet by her mother when she did something wrong. "One time it was because I called my sister 'stupid' and I wasn't allowed to use that word. Another time it was because I stuck my tongue out behind my father's back. My mom would get this look on her face and I knew it was coming, she would grab me by the collar and drag me across the room, open the closet door, and throw me in. It was dark in there and smelled like wet wool. On the bottom of the closet in a box were scarves and hats. Sometimes my mom wouldn't open the door for hours. One time she forgot about me all night and I spent the night on top of three berets and a pair of leather gloves."

⊛✖⊛

The one-wrong-move syndrome is about the fragility you carry in your body, the belief that if things are going well, it is an illusion in the same way as when your alcoholic father showed up sober at the school play and acted like everyone else's father for one night. You were prepared for the worst, you were always prepared for the worst. You knew that things could fall apart at any moment. You knew that things had already fallen apart, but you never stopped hoping for your father to stay sober forever. And you never stopped hoping for your family to be different, and you never stopped pretending that they already were.

Every night, I would turn off the light beside my bed and kneel on the floor, hands cupped in a prayer. *Please God, bless Mom and Dad, but don't let them get a divorce.* Every night for ten years, even after doors slammed and my mother disappeared for two days, I prayed, knowing that I couldn't hold on any more. I was slipping, they were slipping, but I kept hoping, praying. Don't let them get a divorce.

Each summer in camp, a tug of war was staged during the Olympics. The two sides, the Aztecs and the Conquistadores, prepared themselves by placing their strongest people in the front. They dug holes for their heels, they wore gloves to prevent rope burn, they stood next to the rope which lay like a sleeping snake at their feet. And then Hal, the head counselor, blew the whistle and the strong ones picked up the rope and tugged, while the campers, wearing red for Aztecs and blue for Conquistadores, screamed, "Pull, pull, pull harder, harder, pull, pull." In the evening, and by the light of a fire, you could see them getting tired, you could see them slipping from the holes they had dug, you could see that your team was going to lose. But you kept hoping, even as Lee Rordine, the strongest one, his arms bulging and his face locked in gritty determination, scrunched his body and got ready for one last victorious pull, you kept hoping something would happen, please God, don't let them get a divorce.

I was an Aztec child, building an empire on the hope that Lee Rordine would slip at the last moment and drop the rope. My mother stocked the refrigerator with Häagen-Dazs ice cream. I was the only person I knew who could come home from school to six pints of gold and white flavors, and I was sure that had to count for something. Frances and her sister Margaret came over on Sundays just to stand in front of the refrigerator and stare at the crabmeat salad and the fried chicken from the Poultry Mart, the coffee and vanilla and rum-raisin ice cream. We were appreciative lovers gazing at the golden moon bodies of our beloveds. After a few minutes of murmuring and salivating, we chose what we wanted to eat and brought it to the table, eyes gleaming. With each spoonful of food, I chanted in silence: I have a regular family, there is chicken and ice cream in the refrigerator, I am just like you, I am I am I am. If my mom stocks the freezer, she must love me, she must be a regular mom. So what if she is never home? So what if my dad doesn't talk to anyone? This is real, you can see this food, touch it, it is better food than anyone else's mom puts in their refrigerators. My mom is a good mom, a kind mom, she is. A mom who buys Häagen-Dazs can't possible be thinking about leaving, please, God, don't let them get a divorce.

But the layer of illusion was thin as November ice on a pond. Looking at it from the hill, you think you can glide on the pond for hours. But when you test it with your finger, it cleaves open and the layer of ice is swallowed. I layered myself with November frosts: my mom is a regular mom and we are a regular family. I lied to myself, I lied to my friends. I believed my lies.

The more I pretended, the more fragile I became. The more

I pretended, the more likely it was for something, anything, to trigger the underworld of despair I was hiding. The greater the distance between truth and my appearance, the greater the possibility of being knocked off center by one wrong move. Being on a diet and pretending that I loved not eating cheese or chocolate or that it was okay to not be in a room with cake for the rest of my life made it much more likely that I would binge when someone commented on my hair, my dress, the weather. Spending years pretending that I didn't feel anything when my mother left made it much more likely that I felt abandoned when Matt left on a three-day trip. The one-wrong-move syndrome is a symptom of a lifetime of telling lies.

☺✖☺

I was seventeen when I first tried to tell anyone the truth. My friend Penny and I were sitting in Squire's Delicatessen on Middle Neck Road. I had ordered a Weight Watcher's coffee malted and was doodling on the pink linoleum countertop with my finger. My mother had come in at four-thirty that morning; my father left for work at six-thirty. I wanted to grab him by the shoulders and scream at him to do something; I wanted to call my mother an adulteress and tell her that she was breaking one of the Ten Commandments. But I decided instead to tell Penny what I saw and ask her for her advice. Penny was the only friend I had whose mother was divorced, so I assumed she knew about things like adultery.

When my malted and her hamburger came, I said, "Did your mom have an affair while she and your dad were married?"

"Nope," she answered, putting a piece of half-sour pickle in her mouth.

This wasn't going to be easy. I fumbled with the bowl of coleslaw, waggling a strand of carrot from the jumble of mayonnaise and cabbage.

"Well, whaddya mean? I mean, what caused the divorce?"

"I don't know. I guess they were unhappy together."

"Did your mom ever hit you?"

"Nope," she answered again. "Have you seen Jeffrey Etra's new girlfriend? She goes to Roslyn; she's a senior and Sue told me that she went all the way with a boy from college in the back seat of a car! Can you *ba-leeve* that?"

"I think my mom is having an affair," I said quickly.

"Oh, don't be ridiculous. That's the silliest thing I ever heard."

"Yeah, I guess it is," I said, and ate another bite of coleslaw, while I waited for a second coffee malted.

❀✖❀

For the next eighteen years, I became an expert at two potent survival mechanisms: denial and minimization. When I went to India and learned about reincarnation and choosing one's parents, I decided that I needed to grow up in an alcoholic and violent home for my soul to learn its lessons. I forgave my mother. I continued to idealize my father. All was well. Until a few years ago, when I met Matt and suddenly felt like a child again. Each time he left for a trip, each time he got angry at me, my tongue froze in the back of my throat as it tried to form words that were banished thirty years ago. Words like: I'm afraid that when you leave, you will never come back. Words like: Stay with me, I need you, when you get angry, I'm afraid you will kill me.

❀✖❀

The one-wrong-move syndrome is a description of what happens when something or someone triggers the feelings that we never learned words to describe. It is a description of the sudden change we undergo when unconscious and denied feelings rise to the surface and like a swarm of bees, fill the air with noise so thick you feel it will make you insane. It is a result of being an adult and experiencing the present as a child would.

During a workshop I led in Chicago, I asked the participants to describe their childhoods in one or two words. I transcribed a random dozen of their responses: torn-apart, bombed, isolated, lonely, war zone, sad, okay, drunken, violent, Hiroshima-like, tormented. Remember that this was a workshop about breaking free from compulsive eating, not about troubled families, sexual abuse, alcoholism, or battering.

I work with several thousand people a year. I have been leading workshops for twelve years. Most people describe their childhoods in exactly the same way as these dozen participants from Chicago. I say this not to blame the mothers and fathers but to offer an explanation to the adult children: when your childhood was torn apart and you haven't given yourself the opportunity to grieve for the lost years, you see life through the lens of "torn-apart." You see that life is not kind, life is not safe, you can't count on anything. When something is easy—a relationship, a situation— you feel as if you are overlooking something and better not begin thinking that this is the way it will continue. Three years ago, I wrote in my journal, "When I am happy, I question whether I am denying something, and when I am unhappy, I wonder whether I will always be like this."

When you look at the world through a broken lens, the world looks shattered. You carry the vision of imminent catastrophe inside your heart, so that when one thing happens—you get back from a trip and the pot is scorched, you eat a piece of pizza when you aren't hungry—you react with the sorrow and rage of ten thousand years. The pot is scorched and your mother left you and your father abused you and your lover threw a cast-iron frying pan at you and you got thrown in jail for civil disobedience and the dolphins are getting killed for tuna sandwiches and you lost the spelling bee when you were ten because Ricky Petosa pinched your ass. It is not just this moment, it is not just this wrong move, it is all the moments, all the wrong moves when you were hurt and it felt as though everything was lost and nothing would ever be right again. One wrong move and all the unspoken betrayals and resentments, the crushed dreams, the terror of living with a father you had to rescue or a mother you had to mother, one wrong move and every single wrong move that anyone ever made in your life becomes this wrong move, now.

You split yourself into two people: the adult who has nothing to do with the pain and the child who feels nothing but the pain. The adult who functions smoothly and responds appropriately and the child who has stick-out edges and wants to say no to everything, be comforted at all times, stand up and scream for attention in the middle of a quiet auditorium. The child is your witness; the past is indelibly etched, like a cattle brand, in her body. When people get to know you, you feel as if they are not seeing the real you because you know that next week or next month or next year, one wrong move could bring the unfinished past reeling in. You are like a connect-the-dots drawing without the line that connects the dots. You have buried the thread that makes sense of it all and in so doing have given three eclairs the power to ruin your life.

❧✗❧

The one-wrong-move syndrome is a description of the effect that unacknowledged or minimized events in the past have on our daily life. We must go through the past to live in the present. Through, not beyond. Through, not above. Through, not out of. Speaking, feeling, crying, raging, laughing, being fearlessly honest about the past. In this way, the present becomes itself, nothing more. When you eat a frozen pizza because someone at work said you looked like you had put on a few pounds, you haven't proved to yourself, your mother, or your ex-leader from Weight Watchers that you can never lose weight and will be fat and ugly for the rest of your life: you've eaten a frozen pizza. And the next time you get hungry, you will eat again. When you and your lover have a fight and he calls you selfish, it doesn't mean that your mother was right and you are a horrible human being and can never love anyone ever. It means that your lover got angry and called you selfish. And when he is not angry, he will call you Punky again.

CHAPTER
6

Grieving for the Lost Years

I am sitting in the Coconut Room of the Le Baron Hotel in San José with Rose and Deborah; it is two A.M. and I am fifty pounds over my natural weight. I am the fattest I have ever been in my life. It is the third week of my commitment to stop dieting; I have just spent thirteen days eating nothing but chocolate chip cookies—raw and cooked—and·I am terrified that I will gain a hundred pounds, that I will eat nothing but sugar for the rest of my life. I am terrified that the decision to trust myself is permission to binge in disguise, and that the conviction that I can eat what I want is the basis of the worst trick I have ever played on myself.

Rose orders a Greek salad; Deborah orders broiled chicken and zucchini; I order a brownie with vanilla ice cream and hot fudge sauce.

When the waiter puts the brownie in front of me, Deborah says, "I can't believe you are going to eat that! Look at yourself— you're fatter than you've ever been. How can you do that to yourself? It's almost revolting to watch."

I'm a puddle of shame. I want to disappear without a word and I want to eat the table. I hate everything about myself—my stubby fingers, my tree-trunk legs—and I hate Deborah. She's right, this is revolting. *I* am revolting.

The silence is bruising, but I have no idea what to say. It

sounds ridiculous to tell her that eating brownies and ice cream at two A.M. is going to help me lose weight. And I can't tell her to mind her own business; I've never told that to anyone.

I am sitting at the kids' table at Grossinger's Hotel in the Catskill Mountains. The waiter comes to take our orders. Geri orders meat loaf and mashed potatoes, Ricky orders a hamburger, Donald orders fried chicken. I don't like anything on the menu but vegetables. I order the vegetable plate. When the waiter puts the colorful array on my place mat, all the kids start screaming, "Yuck, ooh, vegetables, how disgusting." I send my dinner back and order meat loaf instead.

Deborah is waiting for an answer.

I take a deep breath. I lift my eyes from the melting rim of ice cream, the part I like best, and look at her. She is huffed up. She is ready for a fight. I say, "I have decided not to diet any more. I am giving myself a year to eat what I want without guilt."

Her startled voice drones on. I don't hear her any more. I don't care what she thinks. I eat half the brownie and three bites of ice cream. When I get home, I eat a piece of toast and peanut butter, three handfuls of granola, and a banana. If I pile enough food on top of the shame, maybe I won't feel it any more.

❧✖❧

During that first year of changing my attitudes and behavior toward food, I spent almost every day wondering if I was crazy. Everyone I knew was on a diet. When I told the leader of my Wednesday evening Weight Watchers group that I was taking a leave of absence, she said, "Eating sensibly and watching everything you put in your mouth for the rest of your life—they are the only things that work." I nodded my head, staring at her kelly green silk blouse, her carefully applied gray eye shadow. I wanted her reassurance, I wanted her to tell me how brave I was, I wanted her to wish me good luck.

I gained ten pounds in the first two months, three pounds the next month. During the fourth month my weight stabilized. At the end of the fifth month of not dieting, I was staying at thirteen pounds heavier than the largest I had ever been—and I couldn't decide whether that was a fabulous accomplishment or a dismal failure. Three months before, I wouldn't have believed that it was possible to eat what I wanted and not gain weight, even for a day; on the other hand, I was already fat, so what difference did it make that I was not gaining any more weight?

In a year and a half, I had gone from a size 2 to a size 16. And I was more particular about food than ever before. If I went into a restaurant and they didn't have something that "hummed"* to me—something I knew I wanted without seeing it, hearing about it, or tasting it—I would leave. One evening, Rose and I went to four different restaurants because I couldn't find a hummer. If the bread arrived cold at the table, I would ask the waiter to bring it back to the kitchen and heat it up. When I went out to dinner with my father, I ordered a cup of hot water with lemon. When I visited my mother's house that year, I ate coffee ice cream for breakfast. For the first time in my life, I was asking for what I wanted and I wouldn't let anyone tell me I couldn't have it. No one knew what to say to me, how to talk to me. No one knew what I was doing.

I knew.

On May 16, 1980, the fifth month of not dieting, I wrote, "I am undoing twenty-eight years of brainwashing, of being told that my hungers are bottomless and that I must be vigilant in my attempt at controlling them. I am *not* spineless; I am *not* devouring. I do not need to be afraid of myself. I can—and will—

---

* A hummer is a food you know you want without first seeing it, hearing about it, or smelling it. For a further description of humming and beckoning foods, see *Breaking Free from Compulsive Eating* (New York: Signet, 1984), pages 35–37.

trust myself to embrace what is life-giving and dismiss what will destroy me. I am lovable, I am loving; my choices about food will reflect that, if I give myself a chance."

When I tried telling this to my friends, especially people who were dieting, it was like screaming in a high wind.

❦✖❦

A few weeks ago, Matt told me that when he was a child his mother made him shoes.

"She *made* you shoes? What about Stride-Rite and Buster Brown?"

"I had wide feet; so did our whole family. She found out about Murray's Space Shoes and she made plaster casts of our feet, then made the shoes to fit the casts. I remember the first time I played outside in them. I felt like I was walking on air."

His mother made him shoes.

His mother invited the chess team to play at their house so that Matt would feel his friends were always welcome.

When his best friend Kenny had his wisdom tooth pulled, he wanted to go to Matt's house so that Barbara could take care of him, make him egg custard.

His mother taught him to cook. When he went to college, they sent recipes back and forth. He still makes his mother's cabbage borscht on rainy winter nights.

The only trauma Matt can remember is the night he fell into the toilet bowl when he was three and his parents were having a party and he had to scream very loud so that someone would hear him and pull him out.

I cannot imagine the safety of a life with a mother who made shoes for me. And Matt cannot imagine a life without it.

When I talk to him about grieving for the lost years, when I talk to him about drama and control and compulsion, he nods his head and makes sympathetic murmurs, but he doesn't understand. Not really.

When I talk in a workshop about the need to go back to the beginning, to unlayer ourselves and go back to what is underneath the compulsion, to the pain that shaped it and made it necessary, to the messages we learned about ourselves, I can see the participants stretching to reach me, but they do not yet understand, not really.

It's too late, they say. We're fifty and sixty years old. Isn't it about time we stopped talking about what happened to us when we were twelve?

Yes it is.

It's time we stop talking about it and start doing something about it.

❀✕❀

My mother.

She got all A's for years and then one year, she can't remember why, she stopped caring about school, she stopped caring about herself. I question her about that year.

"Did anything happen that upset you?" I ask.

"No, not that I can remember."

"Mom," I say, taking a guess, "were you ever sexually molested?"

"Yes."

"Yes? Have you ever talked about it? Did you ever tell your mother about it? What happened?"

"No, I never talked about it. It didn't seem like such a big deal. And it happened such a long time ago. What's done is done."

"But *what happened?*"

"We lived in a tenement house in the Bronx, and my cousin Arnold lived underneath us. On Sundays, when he came to visit, he locked me in the bathroom and pulled out his penis, told me to rub it until it got hard and he climaxed. He told me never to tell my mother. And I never did. He was family, she wouldn't have believed me."

"Mom, it must have affected you. It must have made you feel ashamed of your body, as if you were dirty or bad in some way."

We are sitting in what used to be my bedroom, the same room where I called Penny Lithgow and made twenty-one sleepover dates at one time. I didn't like that room. It was decorated with an orange flowered carpet and a built-in, dark brown wall unit with gold chicken wire cabinets. I wanted lace and frills. I wanted white furniture, a canopy bed, a girl's room.

Now it is a cozy family room, plushy sand-colored carpet, pictures of relatives on the walls. In one photograph, a young blond woman with longing in her eyes and questions on her lips is holding a high school diploma; one year later, she married my father.

Five years ago, my mother knocked out the far wall of my bedroom and put a bay window in its place. No traces of orange or disappointment litter the room now. This is the heart of the house, the place to go when you want to talk, nap, read, feel safe. People visit in the living room, they eat in the kitchen, but they live here.

My mother and I are sitting on the beige plaid couches, facing each other. Behind her is a jungle of plants. A spathefillum flower reaches expectantly from a mass of shiny leaves.

She is thinking about the effect of the molestation.

When she describes her childhood, my mother looks like a well-scrubbed eleven-year-old. Legs crossed, cheeks blazing, eyes raised.

"I suppose it must have had some effect, but I honestly don't remember. . . . I was so lonely during those years. . . . I tried to be such a good girl. . . . I would come home from school and no one would be home, my mother was a saleswoman at Macy's, and I would go into the kitchen and eat . . . big hunks of dark bread that my grandma made. . . . I stopped caring about doing well in school, no one ever seemed to notice. . . . My mother was always mad at my sister, she was the bad one, so I tried to be the good one, I never cursed, I always did what she asked, but they never noticed. . . . I was so lonely and I hated being poor, we didn't have enough money, there was never enough money, never enough . . ."

Never enough. Money, food, love.

Never enough love.

So she married the first boy who paid any attention to her, a boy from whom she could never get enough. My father.

"I didn't even realize I was unhappy until I was thirty years old. And suddenly there I was, with a husband who never came home and two children who needed me. But I had nothing to give. All I could think about was getting away from this feeling I had lived with my whole life. The unbearable loneliness. I had to get away. I had to leave. Can't you see that it had nothing to do with you?"

We are both crying. I nod my head yes then I shake it no. "I can see it now, Mom. I couldn't see it then."

"I missed all your growing-up years. I can't even remember what happened during those years. I was taking sleeping pills at night and diet pills during the day. I was drinking. I was in that accident . . ."

The Accident. We are leaving Grossinger's. My father is checking out, paying the bill, I am standing in the parking lot with my mother. She is leaning on a car with her right leg. Ron Macaluso gets in his new silver Thunderbird with the red leather seats and begins driving toward the car my mother is leaning on. He doesn't see her. He drives into her leg, smashes it between his car and the other one. She screams. The scream rips through my body like jagged metal tearing skin bones heart. She falls. Mom, Mom, are you okay? Get an ambulance, she whispers.

On the way to the hospital, I ride with her in the ambulance, talking the whole time. I am afraid she will die if I stop talking.

She is in shock, the doctor says. She will be okay. Her leg is not broken, just bruised. Badly bruised. It needs a year to heal.

That is the year we move to Great Neck. That is the year she spends on sleeping pills. That is the year she crawls out of bed on Saturday afternoon and begs my father to take her for a ride. When she tells the story now, she says that he wouldn't take her. I don't remember that. I remember the drab green wallpaper with gold velvet designs, the midnight smell of darkness in our new house, my mother in her pink nightgown, pleading for a drink of pineapple juice. Whimpering for attention.

I was the new girl in school. An older girl named Betty followed me every day. I used to run for home, turn around and see her following me, making motions with her hands as if to strangle me. I would run inside the house, heart pounding, feeling as if I had done something wrong and Betty was going to punish me— and the first thing I would hear is my mother's pleading voice: "Genie? Genie? Will you get me some pineapple juice?"

I wanted to tell her about Betty. I wanted to tell her about Ron Adelman and Bobby Wilner and Robert Ostropopper who puffed up their faces and waddled every time they saw me, who surrounded the house one Saturday night when no one was home but me and my brother Howard. They yelled for me to let them in. I wouldn't. I kept peeking out the bathroom window to see if they were gone, but they just stood there, yelling. I knew that if I were pretty, if I were thin, they wouldn't treat me like that. But I was ugly and dumb and fat. I wanted to tell my mother but she was reeling in a world of grogginess. There wasn't room for anyone; her pain was a planet of its own.

"You weren't there, Mom. I needed you and you weren't there."

"I know . . . and I'm sorry, darling. I don't know what else to say. After the accident, when I could finally walk, all I could think of was walking away. I didn't have the nerve to get a divorce—my mother had already gotten down on her hands and knees and begged me not to—so I decided that I would stay with your father, but I was so miserable."

❧✖❧

I will never have a happy childhood. I missed it: the love, the acceptance, the feeling that I mattered. I missed it the first time around and I will never get the chance again. I have been railing against that for twenty years. But railing isn't healing. Healing is another story.

❧✖❧

The first step in healing is telling the truth. When you tell the truth, you acknowledge your losses. When you acknowledge your losses, you grieve about them. When you grieve about them, you let go of defining yourself by how much and how badly you've been abused. You begin living in the present instead of living in reaction to the past.

As long as you eat compulsively, your life is about what you eat, how much you eat, how much you weigh, and what you will look like, be like, when you stop eating compulsively. Your pain seems to be about food, willpower, and looking a certain way. But your pain is not about what it seems to be about. And if you don't know what your pain is about, you can't release yourself from it.

❧✖❧

Matt and I saw *Gorillas in the Mist*, a movie about Dian Fossey and her groundbreaking work with gorillas in Africa. When the poachers slaughtered the adult gorillas to sell their heads to rich men for their office walls, I wept so hard that Matt shook me by the shoulders and said, "This is only a movie, Geneen, they're not really killing the gorillas." When the men arrived to take the baby gorilla to the zoo, when the baby gorilla cried as she was being put into a cage, I sobbed and told Matt that I had to leave.

It was their helplessness. I couldn't stand to watch it. I couldn't stand to feel it.

My brother, Howard, says, "I saw what was going on in our family and decided that there was nothing I could do about it; it was much bigger than me, so I disengaged. It was as if I shot my body with Novocaine and lived numb for twenty years."

Not me. I saw what was going on and I rolled up my sleeves. I said, "I can change this. I can make my parents happy together. If I am sweet enough, if I lie to my father for my mother, lie to my mother for my father, lie to both of them about my despair, I know I can create the family I want. I will not be helpless. I will be so good that my mother will be the perfect mother, my father the perfect father. I will not give up. I will never give up."

And I didn't. When my mother yelled at me, left at three P.M. dressed for her lover in red suede and smelling like lavender gladiolas in a funeral parlor, I shut the doors in my eyes, my chest, enclosed myself behind a wall where my feelings could smash like pool balls against one another and no one would hear. Not even me. I was willing to admit feeling helpless about something *I* did—eating, for instance—but I was not willing to feel helpless about something outside of myself. There wasn't any point, I reasoned, in letting myself feel sad or angry or lonely if I couldn't do anything to make it better. I decided to allow myself only feelings I could do something about, feelings I could find a place for in my body, feelings that would be acceptable to my mother and my father.

Instead of feeling the helplessness of a child whose mother was out of control, I believed that my eating was out of control. And not just my eating. My feelings: my need for reassurance, comfort, attention. Instead of feeling the helplessness of a child whose father ignored the hysterics of his wife, did nothing to protect his children, did nothing to ask himself what his part was, I protected him. Made excuses. Said he worked too hard to be bothered by his mean wife. Told myself he loved me more than anything in the world. Shut the doors.

I learned about wildness from her and denial from him. I

became wild about food, wild in my feelings about myself—and I denied that anything was wrong. The wildness and the denial were exquisite protections. I really was helpless. And I was also stuck. I couldn't ask for new parents. I had no choice but to live in that house and survive in any way I could.

The problem is not that I defended myself so well as a child. The problem is in not defending myself as an adult.

It is underneath these exquisite defenses that the roots of compulsion lie. Compulsive eating is a symbolic reenactment of the way in which we distorted our feelings when we began eating compulsively: we swallowed our feelings; we blamed ourselves; we felt out of control; we believed we couldn't get enough. If we allow ourselves to get sidetracked into believing that food is our problem, we will never heal the wounds that we became compulsive to express.

What is the scariest feeling you can imagine?

What can't you stand allowing yourself to feel?

What were the unspoken agreements that you and your family made about acknowledging—or not acknowledging—the truth?

Who was there to listen to and support you?

Who was responsible for the caretaking in the family?

What happened when you were wrong?

These are the questions to ask yourself.

But most of us don't ever get to them because it means we would reexperience the pain of situations we shut out the first time around. Why should we open to them now? Or because we don't believe it is really possible to eat, feel, or live like a normal person. For so long, we've walked around believing that no one understands us. We believe that our problems are different from anyone else's. We don't have a vision of ourselves as whole. We've given up hope. Or we don't get to the right questions because we're still railing against the love we missed in our childhoods. Or because we're still waiting for someone to come and make it better.

As adults, we still want what we didn't receive as children, and we want it in the form we didn't receive it in: another person who loves and cherishes us, someone who is completely responsible for our well-being.

❸✖❸

We lost something that is irretrievable: we lost the chance of going through life with the absolute knowledge that we are lovable. That was our birthright and we never received it. Now we have to work to achieve what some people were given just because they were born to different parents.

Our parents were responsible for us when we were children, but no one is responsible for us when we are adults. If they weren't there the first time around, no one can ever take their place. Not a lover, not a best friend, not a teacher, not a therapist, not a support group, not anyone. Only you. You are the only one who can provide yourself with unconditional love, safety, and constant attention. Only you.

When my mother met Dick, the man she has been married to for the past eighteen years, her life turned pastel turquoise and peach. Instead of storming into a room, she glided in. Instead of snarling at everyone else's happiness, she basked in her own. And even though I was nineteen and living in New Orleans, I remember the relief of thinking that now, now I will have the mother I always wanted. Now that she is happy, she will be there for me. I've waited a long time for this. I waited and now my waiting is over.

But it wasn't. Every time I saw her, I held on for her to say and do what the mother of my dreams says and does: ask me questions, listen to the answers, care about what I care about, remember what I told her the last time we talked. Be engaged in my life.

Sometimes she did. Sometimes she didn't. And each time she didn't, I would get angry all over again. You weren't there, Mom, and I needed you. Need you still. It isn't fair. Matt's mother made him shoes.

Compulsive eaters spend their lives waiting. We say we are waiting to get thin. We are not waiting to get thin. We are waiting for the longing to be stilled. We are waiting to give the burden of ourselves away. We are waiting to feel complete. The crumpled child is still crumpled, waiting for what she never received. And in our unwillingness to listen to her, just as our parents were unwilling to listen to us, we mistake the longing to be loved for the longing to be thin.

It is an enormous, life-altering mistake.

❂✖❂

I attended a panel last year in Berlin called "The Holocaust: Can It Happen Again?" I heard a concentration-camp survivor named Sidney speak about his experience in seven different concentration camps during World War II. He said he was separated from his family and taken to the first camp by the Nazis when he was seventeen; his best friend from kindergarten was taken with him. One day as they were lined up for work duty, the commandant of the camp walked in and asked Sidney's friend why he looked like hell. The boy stood up and said, "I look like hell, Herr Commandant, because I am so hungry. They have given us nothing but dirty potato peels to eat and that was three days ago." The commandant said, "I can't believe that. I told them to feed you. Now, tell me the truth. Why do you look like hell?"

"I tell the truth. I have had nothing to eat since the dirty potato peels three days ago." Again the commandant asked and again Sidney's friend told him that he was hungry and why. After the last time, and with Sidney watching, the commandant took his gun and shot the boy in the head. As he lay dying, the commandant masturbated on his body.

Sidney said that he was able to survive the camps because he imagined himself living to tell the world about it. "I spent every evening picturing what I was going to say when I got out. It became an obsession with me, this need to tell the world what really happened." But when he was released, Sidney said no one wanted to hear. They didn't want to know. They couldn't stand to feel the pain.

Sidney is sixty years old. When I heard him talk, it was only the second time that he had described the horrors of living in a concentration camp. Not even his own children knew any particulars about his past. In fact, most of his talk was on tape, because, he said, "My wife fears for my life if I speak about this again." The trauma is buried so far down that his wife is afraid that feeling it again will destroy him.

In her marvelous book *For Your Own Good* (New York: Farrar, Straus, Giroux, 1983), Alice Miller says that growing up in an abusive family is more harmful than the experience of living in a Nazi concentration camp. Whereas victims in a camp can identify the enemy, form a camaraderie among themselves, and know in every fiber of their beings that what is happening to them is horrible and unjust, children from abusive families are put in impossible situations: they must remain unaware of their suffering. Because of their dependence and because they are innocent and tender, children adore the people who abuse them. The hatred, mistrust, and rage are directed inside toward themselves, not outside toward their parents. As adults, they reenact and perpetuate the abuse in the form of crazy relationships, compulsions, and violence against themselves or others.

We don't pick our behavior out of a hat; compulsive eating doesn't just descend on us. We don't wake up one morning and suddenly want to eat five cheesecakes and three pizzas. While the repressed feelings about disturbing or traumatic events might trigger our descent into food, they do not cause it. We learn to abuse ourselves from being abused.

And while not all compulsive eaters have been abused, every one of us is carrying around pain from our childhoods. As long as this pain remains unconscious, we will continue to act in ways that defeat our conscious intentions. While wanting to lose weight, we will binge until we make ourselves sick; while wanting to be in a relationship that is supportive and loving, we will find ourselves with people who are not capable of acknowledging who we are and what we need; while wanting to excel at a career we find satisfying, we will remain in jobs that bore us and do not use our talents.

❀✖❀

Grieving means telling the truth to yourself about what you have lost. Speaking the unspeakable. Not protecting anyone from the complex being that you are. If you have lived your life as a "nice" person, someone who takes care of others and never makes waves, telling the truth can be terrifying. Most of us lie, pretend, or hide because we learned very early that revealing ourselves creates distance, whereas pretending and hiding foster the illusion of intimacy.

No one wanted to listen to Sidney tell about his years in the concentration camps. They didn't want to feel the horror of his starving day after day, eating nothing but a handful of dirty potato peels, and watching his best friend get shot in the head. They didn't want to reach that far. They didn't know what they would find if they did.

At age thirty or forty or fifty, no one wants to feel that vulnerable ever again. Like Sidney, we shut our pasts into a room, lock the door, and tell ourselves that what's gone is gone. Like Sidney's wife, we are afraid for our lives if we tell our stories now, after so many years.

❀✖❀

In a recent workshop, a man said, "I eat for the same reason my alcoholic friend drinks."

"What reason is that?" I asked.

"For the pain."

"What would happen if you let yourself feel this pain?"

"Well, as my alcoholic friend says: 'It's not a matter of whether I take this drink or not; it's a matter of whether I jump off this *bridge* or not.' "

People come to Breaking Free workshops to learn how to lose weight and end their obsession with food. I tell them to eat when they are hungry and to stop when their bodies have had enough. You can cure compulsive eating by following some basic guidelines, such as filling your house with the foods you love, listening to your body, learning ways to nourish yourself besides eating.

Curing compulsive eating is the easy part, I say. Take the obsession away and you are still left with the wounds it was designed to blot out. Take the obsession away and you are left feeling as trapped as a child in a family where there is no one to turn to and nowhere to go but off a bridge. An obsession freezes your feelings in time; when you transfer the pain of being alive to the pain of being fat, it is as if the delicate clock of your emotional development gets splintered on concrete. If you were sexually abused at the age of five, told no one, and began eating compulsively, you will be left with the raw terror that you felt at five when, at age forty-six you stop using food to comfort yourself. Unless you do something with terror or sadness or rage, with feelings of abandonment or engulfment, with messages you received and internalized about your self-worth and lovableness, unless you bring them to the surface where you can look at them, turn them over and decide if and where they belong now, they stay rooted to the childhood soil in which they were planted.

Feelings do not go away just because they have no relevance to our present situations. Like shadows that disappear when you face them, feelings disappear when you name them, and only then.

Grieving is a process that involves denial, blame, anger, loss, desolation, exhaustion*, and—ultimately—acceptance of the wounds, the betrayals, the fact that no one can kiss it and make it better. Grieving about the past is not something you do against your parents; it is something you do for yourself, although confronting one's parents can be an essential part of healing for some people.

Nor is grieving to be confused with forgiving those who hurt you. Many people want to fly past grief into forgiveness because grief is so uncomfortable and forgiveness is so sweet. Grieving looks self-indulgent; forgiveness looks holy. But there is nothing holy about faking your feelings, and unless you are willing to get angry with the person or people who hurt you so that you absolutely know you did not deserve their abuse, forgiveness will be a sham. You cannot forgive anyone with whom you never got angry.

Grieving for the lost years is a courageous act because it takes time and we are used to moving fast. Grieving can seem like a full-time job, and with a family to care for, work to report to, and a life that demands our presence, it's hard to believe that we can make room for something as big as grief. Grieving is courageous because it looks like wallowing; in a culture that values success and achievement, we believe we have more important things to do than cry over something that happened thirty years ago. Grieving is courageous because while we are in the middle of it, it seems as if it will never end. Most of all, grieving takes courage because we have no idea what comes after grief.

The purpose of grieving is not just to heal. It is not just to understand the pain. It is not just to forgive or to accept it. Healing is the step between grieving and growing. The purpose of healing is to become whole, and the purpose of being whole is to move

---

* See *The Courage to Heal* (New York: Harper & Row, 1988), by Ellen Bass and Laura Davis, pages 57–59, in which they describe the healing process.

toward a vision of life in which you are fully alive, connected to what sustains you, available to receive and give love. Healing from the past is the first step. Living in the present is the next. Creating a future that preserves clean air and water, trees and birds, cheetahs and dolphins, elephants and whales, rain forests and clouds is the next.

❧✗❧

When I stopped dieting and began eating according to the needs of my body, no one believed I had the audacity to live in such a manner. In the past few years, when I have made a commitment to tell the truth about my past, I watch friends, even those whom I love dearly, wince and wait for me to stop when, in the course of a conversation, something triggers an old hurt and I describe it.

Even Matt has a hard time. A few nights ago at dinner, I asked him about his bar mitzvah. He told me that instead of going to Hebrew school like all his friends, he went to a Workmen's Circle school to learn Yiddish. Instead of getting bar mitzvahed on Saturday like his friends, he was bar mitzvahed on Thursday morning so that his Orthodox grandparents, who couldn't travel on Saturdays, could be there.

"Did you feel funny about being different from your other friends?"

"No, not at all," he said. "It didn't make any sense to have the bar mitzvah on a day that my grandparents couldn't come."

"But that sounds like an adult talking," I said, "not a thirteen-year-old kid who isn't particularly rational."

His eyes flashed and he drew a deep breath. I waited. "You know something, Geneen, not everyone in the world thinks that talking about buried childhood feelings is scintillating dinner conversation. Did it ever occur to you that this fascination with the dark side of life is not particularly healthy?"

Fascinated with the dark side? Am I really fascinated with darkness? Visions of myself wallowing in pain, globs of it stuck to my hair, webbing my fingers and toes. A woman in a workshop told me that her husband accused her of crying when she took out the garbage because she would never see it again. Is that how I seem to Matt?

Matt was waiting for my answer. "If I am fascinated with the dark side, as you call it, that's because the dark side has had so much power in my life. It's what I haven't recognized and felt that has dictated so many of my feelings about myself and my work and my relationships. The more I move the dark side into consciousness, the less pull it has on me. I don't like mucking around in the pain, but I'm willing to do it because it's the only way I know to become whole. And who knows what would happen then? Perhaps I would become the kind of person who would make my children shoes."

⊜✖⊜

My mother never allowed herself to acknowledge the suffering she felt as a child. My father isn't even aware that he suffered. Instead of expressing their pain, they passed it on.

After I finished the second chapter of this book, I read it to Matt. He was visibly moved. Then he said, "But what is your mother going to say about this? What about your father?"

What indeed? I kept telling myself that when I finished writing the first draft, I could go back and change all the stories about my parents; I could use someone else's name. No one would ever know. I wanted to protect my parents; their lives are different now. I wanted to protect myself; I was afraid they might never talk to me again after reading this book.

When I sent my mother and Dick the galleys for *Feeding the Hungry Heart*, Dick called and said, "You can't include that piece about your mother, Geneen, it's not fair. It happened so long ago; we have new friends now who don't even know about that time in her life. You're going to bring it all up again. It's not fair. That's my wife you're talking about."

"Dick," I said quietly, "that's my mother I'm writing about. And I'm sorry if it's going to bring it all up again, but I'm writing about it because for me it never went away."

I don't want to hurt my parents. I want to be with them—and myself—in the fullness of the present. I want to let go of the suffering, not wear it as a banner for the rest of my life. But the only way I know to do that is to acknowledge and grieve about the feelings I locked away the first time around. It seems to me that suffering becomes a banner when you spend your life reacting to it instead of acknowledging it and letting it go.

If I changed all the stories so that they belonged to someone else, the healing would belong to someone else as well. If I pretended that what happened to me did not really happen to me, I would be underscoring my belief that being loved means being hidden. I would be perpetuating my shame about growing up in my family. And I would unwittingly pass that shame on to my children and they, on to theirs.

Where does it end?

With me. With you.

When we decide the time is now.

CHAPTER
7

Being a Victim,
Being Powerful

I am sipping a glass of orange juice. My mother and Dick are eating oatmeal, Matt is drinking Lemon Balm tea. We are sitting in the breakfast room of the Claremont Hotel in Berkeley; it is the Sunday after Thanksgiving and we are meeting one last time before my mother and Dick leave for New York.

"Geneen," Dick says suddenly, "let's you and I go for a walk. I'd like to talk to you."

My stomach tightens, heart pounds. I don't want to go. I know what he wants to talk to me about: He wants to tell me not to write about my childhood in this new book. I feel like a little girl being dragged away from company because she has been bad. I consider telling him that if he wants to talk to me, he can do it here at the table with everyone present. Because I don't have the courage, I say, "Okay, let's go."

We walk past the buffet table piled with fruit: wedges of watermelon, slices of papaya, banana crescents. Dick puts his arm around my shoulders. "Geneen," he says, "Ruth tells me you are writing about your childhood and—"

I recoil from his touch.

"—and I have to tell you, I am very disturbed. You wrote about her once—why do you have to do it again? Do you realize how much you will make her suffer? Can't you think about anyone but yourself?"

I want to scream at him, run back to the table. I protected her throughout my childhood; now he wants me to protect her again. No. I won't do it. No no no.

I try to speak but my voice doesn't work.

Dick goes on: "If you have to write about it, fine, but then burn what you write. Why do you have to shame your mother?"

I tell myself that I have to glue my voice together. Now.

"I'm not writing for the purpose of shaming her, Dick. I'm writing because I want to heal myself and get on with my life, and because I want other people to know that they can do the same."

"I can understand having a problem, so resolve it, but don't write about your mother. Something awful might happen to her if you do."

"Like what?"

"She might have a nervous breakdown. You have to ask yourself if you will be able to put your head on the pillow at night knowing that your book caused this."

We are sitting in the lobby of the hotel in oversized armchairs covered in rose fabric with periwinkle flowers. I trace one of the flowers over and over with my index finger. I am angry, confused, frightened. I think he is overreacting, but what he is saying seems so unreal that I wonder if it might be true. A nervous breakdown.

"Dick, I understand that you have strong feelings about what I am doing. I expected that. I'm not doing this to hurt you, but I'm not going to stop doing it to make you happy. Let's go back to the table."

"All right, Geneen. I just felt like I had to say what was on my mind. I couldn't live with myself if I didn't."

I nod and begin walking back to the dining room. Past the bell captain who has been staring at us for ten minutes, past the wedges of fruit, the sticky buns, the donuts.

I see Matt and my mother from across the room. They are

deep in conversation. Matt is nodding his head—tiny nods, unconscious nods. His eyes are wide and unblinking, his face is alive with attention. I recognize that expression: every muscle in his body looks as if it was put there for the purpose of receiving my mother in this conversation.

When I reach the corner of the table, I touch his shoulder. Matt looks up at me. "Hi. I'm glad you're back." I want to climb into his eyes, sleep in safe waters. He extends his arm to include me in their circle. Dick walks up behind my mother. I am silent. My mother looks at me and says, "You're very upset, aren't you?"

My voice breaks open with tears. "I am. I am." I turn to Dick. "You could have said all of that in front of Matt and Mom. Why couldn't they hear what you said?"

My mother begins to cry, too, tears streaking her face. Smudging her mascara.

"I was afraid that Ruth would get more upset."

"I told him I didn't want him to talk to you," my mother began, "I told him I could handle it myself."

"He thinks you are going to have a nervous breakdown if I publish what I am writing."

"A nervous breakdown? Dick, are you kidding?"

"I simply said that I didn't know what would happen if she published what she is writing." Dick turned to me. "In my world, Geneen, family comes first. Honor your family. The Ten Commandments tells you to honor thy mother and father and I believe that. I live by that. Families are sacred. You don't do anything to hurt the people in them *no matter what*."

He is speaking like a man who believes that parents are always right and children are always wrong. Is he crazy? Am I?

Matt takes my hand and gently squeezes it. He kisses me on the cheek. He looks at Dick and says, "She *is* honoring her mother, Dick. That is exactly what she is doing, but she is honoring her in the best way she knows how: by telling the truth.

Her intention is not to hurt Ruth but to clear the way for their relationship so that they can live in the present moment with each other instead of constantly reacting to the past."

"But why does she have to write about it?"

Matt says, "Have you ever seen the letters she gets from people who've read her books? Most of them come from people who say Geneen is the only one who understands what they've been through because she's willing to write about feelings that most people consider shameful. This isn't about hurting anyone, Dick—it's about helping many, many people."

My mother pulls her attention away long enough to look at her watch. "I'm so sorry we have to leave like this, but we're going to miss our plane if we stay much longer. We still have to finish packing." She looks at me and says, "When we talked about this yesterday, I understood what you said. I understood your need to write about this and I know we'll work everything out, I know that between us, we will deal with our feelings and come to a place that feels good. I have faith in you and in me, I really do. I love you, sweetheart."

"I love you, too, Mom."

The four of us face each other. I keep my eyes focused above Dick's head. "I'm sorry if I upset you, Geneen, but it was better to say it than kick myself for not speaking up two years down the line."

"Uh-huh," I say. "Bye, Mom. I'll call you in a day or two."

"Take care of my baby," she says to Matt as the elevator doors close.

∞✖∞

When I was seven and living in Bunk 6 at Camp Towanda for the summer, I was the jacks champion of the lower division. With a Spaulding ball and my navy blue jacks, I could beat anyone, even Susie Kleiner, at Chicken in the Coop, Flying Dutchman, and Cherries in the Basket. On a drizzly July day in

Honesdale, Pennsylvania, Lebanon Fadish challenged me to a game; I accepted. The game started innocently enough but when we got to Flying Dutchman, Lebanon dropped a jack and I said it was my turn. She said she hadn't meant to drop the jack and it wasn't my turn. I said it was and then she stood up. I stood to face her. Lebanon had thousands of freckles, wiry hair, and beady eyes with orange flecks. She had a brother named Randy and a mother who showed up on visiting day in fluorescent yellow stretch pants and earrings with plastic bananas hanging from them. Lebanon's nickname was "Radish"; mine was "Genie Bikini." Standing there looking at her, I watched her lips crease and her mouth get white; when her eyes narrowed, I was struck by how monstrous she looked. In the next moment, she extended her right arm behind her in a wide swing and then cracked it across my face. I was stunned. I put both my hands on my burning patch of face and stood there, staring.

Bunk 6 gathered around us in a circle, waiting to see what happened next. "Smack her back," Melanie hissed. "Give her what's coming to her." "Kick her in the ass," Betty cheered. They waited. And they waited. In a minute or two, hands still on my face, I walked to my bed, lay down, and covered myself with an army-green blanket. I turned my face away from Lebanon and Helaine and Melanie. Twenty minutes later, when I was sure no one was looking, I grabbed the package of Switzer's red licorice from my cubby, walked through the back door, and sat beneath the bathroom window, eating and crying. Afterward, I told myself that I was a fat slob and it was no wonder Lebanon hit me. But before I fell asleep that night, I replayed the incident over and over. This time I hit her back. This time I sat on her face as I screamed one word over and over again: Rat-ish, Rat-ish, Rat-ish.

❧✖❧

When I was eight and living in the black-and-white house on Eightieth Street, my mother once hit me with a stick. We were standing on the stairs; she was angry, she was yelling, she sounded just like Marian Smokman next door, whose shrieks we could hear through the wall, between twitches of Samantha's nose on "Bewitched" or Kitten crying on "Father Knows Best." Marian was five feet tall with a belly that protruded from her daily uniform of pedal pushers and jungle print blouses. She wore purple lipstick that extended past her lips, past the dark mustache above her mouth, almost to her nose. Marian's husband, Norman, had planted a flagpole in their front yard, and every day before school, even in the snow, Marian, wearing a splashy mu-mu, hoisted the flag. When John Kennedy died, she kept it at half-mast for six months. Every time we heard her screaming at Joe or Bobbi or Judy, my mother would say, "Poor kids," and I would imagine those lips getting bigger with sounds as big as couches hurling from them.

My mother was mad at me because I had crossed Ditmars Boulevard by myself. I was shrinking away from her, walking backward up the stairs. She had a long stick in her hand. I was watching the stick, her face, the stick. When I reached the top step, she swung the stick back and then cracked it on my shoulder. Once, twice. Three times. I cried, pleaded with her to stop. Later that day, I tiptoed down the stairs to the living room, where she was sitting in the black-and-white armchair doing a crossword puzzle. Her legs were folded beneath an orange-and-pink mohair blanket. She looked up when she saw me. Mom, I whispered, bending down on my knees—her mouth was creased in a thin line, her eyes were focused on my mouth—you can hit me anytime you want but please don't use a stick again.

I made myself sick. I hated myself for pleading with her, for telling her it was fine to hit me. Later, in my room, I decided that I was never going to humiliate myself that way again.

I didn't cry in front of my mother for the next twenty years. I didn't want to give her the satisfaction of knowing she had hurt me. I decided that if I could wall my feelings in, if I didn't flinch when she touched me, if I didn't talk to her when she yelled at me, I would maintain a shred of dignity. I would never be reduced to begging again. Let her hit me with a stick. I wouldn't talk to her, I wouldn't blink my eyes. I wouldn't love someone who didn't love me.

Each time I felt a storm brewing in the house, I gathered myself from the parts of my body I was occupying at the moment—my hands and legs, my face, my arms—and I made myself small enough to fit into a pocket of my chest.

When the eruption came, I stood very still, waited until she was done, and when she told me to go to my room and not come out until I was ready to apologize, I walked away quickly. Once inside my room, I wept. Often, I ate Hydrox cookies and wept or ate Milky Ways and wept. Food and tears. Tears and food. Alone in my bedroom where no one could see me, I did all my crying and most of my eating. Later in the day, I talked, moved, did homework, watched TV—but the parts of me that really mattered weren't there and my mother couldn't touch me.

❧✖❧

When I was thirty-five and living in the house on Audrey Street, when I first met Matt and we were fighting about something, anything, I gathered myself into a corner of myself, walled myself behind my face, looked but stopped seeing, spoke in a cardboard voice, arms limp. First he asked me not to withdraw. I said nothing. Then, in a loud voice, he asked me again not to withdraw. But by that time, I was so far away that his voice sounded as if he was speaking to me through water. Once he stopped the car in the middle of Soquel Avenue and I opened the door and walked out. A car shrieked to a halt, I kept walking. I didn't look back. I didn't know him any more.

Time after time, we had a fight and I retreated to a corner he couldn't see, couldn't touch. One night he got so angry with my silence that he started hitting the steering wheel; I looked straight

ahead of me, read the sign on Larry and Edy's Buckwagon restaurant: Hamburgers and Fishsticks: $6.95; I wondered what Edy
looked like, how long they had been married. Matt started
screaming: I can't *stand* it when you do this. I said nothing. But
I thought, He's just like my mother. How did I wind up with
someone who is just like my mother? I don't like him. He scares
me, yelling like that. Next thing you know, he's going to try to
hit me; I'll kill him if he lays a hand on me. I don't want to
spend my life with him, he's a maniac. As soon as we get home,
I'm going to tell him to leave.

Anyone who yelled at me couldn't love me and I wasn't about
to love someone who didn't love me.

❀✖❀

My mother led Howard and me to believe that her pain was our
fault. We believed her. The abusive way she translated her despair, the fact that she tossed her pain like garbage to her children,
was her fault. She should have known better.

But if I am still crying in a bag of Switzer's red licorice, if I
am still crushing myself in a silent corner, if I walk out in the
middle of traffic on Soquel Avenue, if Matt leaves me because
I won't talk to him, it's not her fault. I should know better. And
if I don't know better, then I should find a way to learn.

At some point in my life, my pain has to stop being about
abuse and abandonment. At some point in my life, I have to
move from being the child of a drug-dependent mother to being
a woman who is connected to the source of her own vitality and
who is responsible for the ways she chooses to ignore it or
express it.

❀✖❀

A victim is someone who has no choices, someone who is dependent on those around her to protect her. A victim's sense of
well-being, or lack of it, comes from the love, or lack of it, she

receives from her environment. A victim looks outside, not in-side, herself for clues about her feelings, her next move. Children are victims. If a child is wounded, abused, violated, the best she can do is figure out how to thread herself among the wounds, abuse, violations—and survive despite them.

We were not responsible for the drunkenness, the unpredict-ability, the dishonesty. We were not responsible if we grew like a twisted plant reaching for a shaft of light in a darkened room. We didn't know better. But then, neither did our parents. They too grew up with parents who thought that children were always wrong and parents were always right, that children should be seen and not heard. Many of them grew up waiting for someone to toss them a scrap of dignity. Our fathers were molested by uncles, soldiers, teachers; our mothers were taught to mistrust their bodies, to have babies, to put themselves last. Child abuse was rampant, but no one talked about it. Alcoholism was wide-spread but tolerated, revered as manly or regarded as funny. When a man hit a woman, he was putting her in his place, she deserved it. Our parents were victims, too. So were their parents. Everybody is somebody's baby.

We are not to blame for what happened to us as children, but we are responsible for what we do with our pain as adults. At some point in our lives, we've got to stop being somebody's neglected baby.

❂✖❂

When a compulsive eater hears that instead of dieting she can eat what she wants, her first reaction is usually to rejoice like the Munchkins when they learned that the Wicked Witch was dead. Relief. Freedom. Exhilaration. A diet or food plan is similar to an oppressive, authoritarian parent who tells you what to do and when to do it. Diets perpetuate the child in each of us who was treated with mistrust and restrictions. Diets keep us focused out-side ourselves—on what we are allowed to eat, when we are allowed to eat it, and how much of it we are allowed to have at one sitting. Diets keep us dependent on a source outside ourselves—the diet itself—for our sense of well-being and self-worth.

When we are good and follow the diet, we praise ourselves the way our parents praised us when we looked both ways before crossing the street. When we are bad and go off the diet, we scold ourselves the way our parents scolded us when we stole our sister's Betsy Wetsy doll. Diets restrict our choices and perpetuate our dependence. Many people are comfortable on diets because the feelings they experience while on and off a diet are the same feelings they've experienced about themselves their entire lives.

A child who has been abused believes it is her fault; a person who goes on a binge believes she lacks self-control. Instead of getting angry at her abuser, the child gets angry at herself. Instead of refusing to go on another diet ever again, the compulsive eater punishes herself for bingeing and goes on another diet.

With a diet, the anger and humiliation stay forever self-directed. Diets and food plans enable adults to remain children, victims of oppressive familial and cultural systems in which they spend their lives punishing themselves for not being good enough.

So they come to a Breaking Free workshop and I tell them to eat what they want when they are hungry. And after the initial rejoicing, they tell me they can't do it. Their jobs have restricted meal breaks, how can they eat when they are hungry, how can they eat just chocolate for dinner or how can they eat pizza when their spouses are on low-cholesterol diets? How can they afford to eat what they want when they are already too fat?

But those aren't the real reasons. The real reasons are that if they begin to be kind to themselves around food, if they actually let themselves have what they want and *do not punish themselves afterward*, then their fathers and mothers, their teachers, their lovers, everyone who treated them with mistrust, anyone by whom they were violated or abused, everyone about whom they have an investment in not recognizing the truth, will have been wrong. In discovering that they are worth being kind to, worth living with in compassion and abundance, they unfold softly into a journey of self-discovery that changes their lives forever.

When we experience the body knowledge that no one knows what's better for us than we ourselves do, a seed of autonomy and self-responsibility is planted. Relationships change—with parents, with lovers, with eating buddies, wherever denial and lies were part of the unseen fabric of the connection. Once you experience even the palest glimmer of self-love, it becomes increasingly difficult to feel comfortable in relationships where all that exists is the pretense of love.

It's not as if you wake up one day and decide to stop visiting your parents in Florida; and it's not as if you are eating dinner with your spouse and in the middle of the mashed potatoes decide that you need a few weeks apart. The changes don't happen suddenly. And they don't necessarily involve separations or endings; they involve telling the truth to yourself and then deciding how to live according to that truth.

Breaking free from compulsive eating is a process, but it's a radical process because it asks that you stop being a victim. It gives you choice, self-responsibility. It asks that you stop waiting for someone to make you better.

Breaking free from compulsive eating means going against a culture that encourages us to define our self-worth according to externals—what we look like, how much we weigh, how much money we make. A dress manufacturer said, "We're selling love, not dresses. If we can convince the buyer that our merchandise will bring them love, we've done our job well." Fat is a multibillion-dollar industry. Diet centers and weight-loss programs are getting richer and fatter as they convince us that we should be thinner and thinner. No one in the weight-loss industry wants to see us breaking free.

But mostly, breaking free is hard because as little as we have now, at least we have *something*. Change is frightening, even if it's change that empowers us. An abusive mother is better than no mother. A loveless relationship is better than no relationship. On a television program about adult children of alcoholics, a woman in the audience said that even if her relationship with her mother involved lying, at least she *had* a relationship. And she was not willing to risk losing it by telling the truth. Confronting one's parents is not a necessary part of healing. But if she is not telling the truth because she believes she needs her relationship with her mother to survive, then she is living her life as a child victim.

When compulsive eaters tell me that they can't possibly follow the eating guidelines because their spouses are on a diet or their kids have to eat meat loaf three times a week, when they say, more or less, that their eating is someone else's fault, I answer that there are many things in life beyond our control, but our eating is not one of them; it *is*, however, a perfect reflection of what we believe about responsibility, autonomy, and blame. We must name what we are speaking about. We must be specific. At an earlier time in our lives, when we had no choices and were completely dependent on our environment, the quality of our lives was beyond our control. We must redirect the anger, place it outside us, not bury it inside us with ice cream.

The act of breaking free from compulsive eating by breaking free from diets, rules, food plans, and the ensuing self-punishment enables you to stop being a victim in one very important area of your life. The skills you develop as you break free teach you that your body is good, your instincts are wise, you have many choices, you can rely on yourself for the information you need to live lovingly.

The willingness to embark on this journey and the perseverance to follow through with it take courage and commitment. Compulsive eaters would have to stop blaming everything that is wrong in their lives on their weight. And that's a tall order because many of us developed compulsive eating as a way to blame ourselves for the pain in our lives. If every time my mother hit me I ate a bag of Milky Ways and felt fat and ugly, I could easily justify her actions: my mom hits me because I am fat and ugly. My mom is not crazy; my mom knows what she is doing; my mom knows what is best for me. Compulsive eating was my way of keeping my love for my smart and beautiful mother intact. I couldn't blame her—she was my mother, I needed her—and, in an interaction in which only two people were involved, that left me with only one person to blame: myself. Blaming myself helped me to construct a framework in which I understood what was happening. It allowed me to believe that since I was doing something (eating too much, being selfish) to *make* her hit me, I could change what I was doing (lose weight, be kinder) to make her stop.

The problem with blame is that it focuses our attention on the person with whom we are dealing instead of on ourselves. The more we focus on what the other person is doing, has done, can do, to make us feel better, the less powerful we feel. Revenge fantasies have their place in the healing process: wanting to hurt the person who hurt us can be an indication that we are willing to fight for and protect ourselves. But healing and growing whole eventually require focusing on ourselves and assuming responsibility for change.

I spent so many years not getting angry, so many years betraying myself, telling lies—you can hit me anytime you want, Mom, just don't hit me with a stick—so many years feeling helpless and devastated and believing it was all my fault that getting angry and blaming someone else, instead of withdrawing into a corner of myself and saying nothing, was a major accomplishment. Getting angry is crucial to healing. And just as important is to act on the choice I have as an adult that I didn't have as a child: to protect myself, to establish clear boundaries about what I will and won't tolerate, to know that I do not have to stay in a relationship with a person who does not honor my feelings, to express my hurt or anger—without blaming someone else.

❂✖❂

Six summers ago, I was living alone in a house that was built for charm and quaintness; when I locked my keys inside the door, I had to pry the back window open with a nail file. If a nail file or pen was not available, I twisted two nails that were keeping the bathroom windows in place and I climbed in. I loved that house, loved the way the sun flooded the kitchen, loved the view of the gardens from the bedroom and the kitchen and the bathroom, loved the cherub statues emerging from the ivy. As you entered the house, a glass wall revealed the back yard: delphiniums and plum trees in summer, bushes that looked like strings of tiny pumpkins in fall and winter, carpets of forget-me-nots in spring, and in every season the washes of green: moss green, emerald green, lime green. While I was living in that house, a strawberry-blond man in his early thirties, a man with freckles on his nose and the back of his hands, a man with smile crinkles around his eyes, the sort of man you might look at and say, "Oh, what a kind face," this man raped nine women in four months and was last seen at the end of my block.

The first rape occurred in April. By July, the women of Santa Cruz were gathering at weekly town meetings in the bakery at the East Cliff Village Shopping Center. Members of the police department, Men Against Rape, Women Against Rape, mothers, daughters, lovers, spouses, friends, we were all frantic in our attempts to educate ourselves, trying to figure out what we could do to stop this man, and what we, as women, would do if we were awakened at three A.M. by a man with a stocking over his head who said, "Don't move, cunt, or you're dead meat."

Ellen said she would knock his teeth out of his mouth, gouge his face with her nails. "I would turn my house upside down if

I had to, but he would be sorry he ever came near me." Judith said she would kick him in the balls, bite him wherever she could, but one thing she knew for sure: he would never harm her or her daughter. Never.

I was silent during these outpourings. I hadn't slept more than two straight hours in four months; every time the floor creaked or the refrigerator hummed or a cat knocked over a garbage can, I jumped from my bed and ran to the back door, opened it, and began running outside. By the time I reached the garden, I realized that the rapist was not in the house and I could go back inside. I repeated this scenario two, three, four times each night. Once, when I thought I heard him in my study, I reached for the phone and dialed 911. Another night, I called Sara at twelve-thirty, telling her that I thought he was in my house. I woke up six or seven times a night. I ran outside at two, three, and four in the morning. I was cellophane-sheer, hanging on by claws.

Then Cliff reminded me of the self-defense class he had read about the previous spring, the one in which a male instructor dressed in sixty-five pounds of padding, acting as an assailant, attacks you and doesn't stop attacking you until you deliver a "knock-out blow"—a blow that would knock out anyone who wasn't wearing the padding. I remembered the description of the class well. When Cliff showed me the picture in the paper of the padded instructor, my body began to tremble. His helmet was bigger than a giant pumpkin with two holes cut out for the eyes. He looked like Darth Vader inflated with rock-hard helium and I didn't want to go near him. Besides, I reasoned at the time, violence begets violence. If I start thinking violent thoughts, I will attract violent men. When I told my friend Lisa about the course, she said, "You can stop violence with love. Elisabeth Kübler-Ross once stopped a raging elephant in her path by casting love in its direction." Yeah, I said to myself, love can change anything. Except that when I woke at two, three, and four, love was not my predominant emotion. The most frightening aspect of my imagined encounter with the rapist was what I imagined I would do if he entered my house:

Three A.M.: I awaken from the noise of the front door being pushed open. I jump out of bed, and in the dark I make out a man with a stockinged head coming toward me. He says, "Don't move." And I don't. Gathering myself into a corner of myself, I remove any traces of caring from my body. I lie there, doing nothing, saying nothing, frozen to the red-tile floor while he fumbles with my flannel nightgown, sticks his penis inside me, rapes me. Horrified and confused by this vision, I tell Ellen that I will enroll in the Model Mugging class with her.

The first night of the class was terrifying. And the second and the third, the fourth. The fifth. Every time the instructor attacked me, I froze or I cried or I froze and I cried. Eventually, with enough coaching from the female instructor and the women in the class, I learned to fight back. Then I graduated from the course and enrolled in the intermediate course: two assailants on one woman. My friends called me a masochist. My chiropractor told me my back was suffering from the side kicks and the scissor kicks and the knee-to-the-groin kicks. But the fear was encrusting me like lava and I knew I had to break through it. The third week of the course, as I was pinned by one man and (supposedly) being raped by another, I stopped fighting. My arms went limp, my legs stopped kicking. I gave up. For the first time in my adult life, I remembered walking backward up the stairs, I remembered the years of standing in front of my mom with my hands at my sides knowing that if I fought back, I'd get hit harder.

The instructor's silver braid rests on my cheek. From the corner of my eye, I can see the tip of her red shoe.

"Look at me," she says, "listen to me," she says. "You've got to fight, Geneen. They are hurting you."

"I don't care what they do. I can't fight back. I don't care what they do to me. It's too hard, they're too strong."

I begin to weep, loud rasping cries. One of the men gags

me with a red scarf, the other ties my hands behind my back.

Danielle, the instructor, says, "I don't know who hurt you so badly, Geneen, but whoever it was was wrong. No one ever has permission to violate someone else. Ever. It wasn't your fault. Now, get up and stop them from hurting you more."

I still don't move. I think, This will be over soon. Then I can rest. I hear the men speaking to each other. "She's not fighting back, Mario. We can do anything we want to this cunt."

Danielle holds my face and points it toward her. "You're waiting for them to stop, Geneen. You think if you're sweet enough or weak enough or kind enough they will stop. You think you can get them to change their minds, as if their behavior has anything to do with the kind of person you are.

"You've got to stop waiting, Geneen, you've got to stop waiting for them to stop. *You've* got to stop *them*."

I hear the rest of the women in the class screaming instructions from the sidelines: Get on your side, they yell, kick him in the groin, put your fingers in his eyes. C'mon, Geneen, Danielle says, stop them *now*.

I jump up, work my hands out of the rope, move closer to the tall man. He grabs my shoulders. I step toward him with my left leg, kick him in the groin with my right leg. He doubles over, I pound his head with my elbow, he falls to the ground. The other man is circling me, grabs me by the waist, throws me to the ground. I kick him in the chest, he falls back. I move closer, kick him in the head, he falls back again. I keep kicking, I aim for his chest his head his groin. He gives the "knock-out" signal and the whistle blows.

In Model Mugging, * I learned that in order to deal effectively with someone who was violating me, I couldn't let myself be distracted by what he was doing. As soon as I began focusing on

---

* For more information about Model Mugging, you can write Model Mugging of SLO, Box 986, San Luis Obispo, CA 93406, or call 800-345-KICK.

his intentions, his movements, his words, my power leaked away. If I managed, despite the presence of two 6′4″ thugs, to stay in touch with my body, with my resolve to protect myself, with my conviction that no one had the right to violate me and anyone who tried would receive the full force of my rage, I could use my fear to fight like a Bengal tiger whose cub has been threatened.

In real life, especially in the presence of weapons, it is not always possible or wise for rape victims to fight back. The lesson of Model Mugging is not that victims of sexual assault who don't fight back are weak or in any way to blame but that as adults, we have a choice in any situation. Choosing *not* to fight is a choice that could save your life. But it must be recognized as a choice. Victims stop being victims the moment they recognize their power to choose.

And the lesson of Model Mugging is that we cannot be kind enough or thin enough or generous enough, we cannot be successful enough or attractive enough for those who abuse us to stop abusing us. We cannot make anyone love us. We cannot change anyone. It is not our job to hurt someone who has hurt us, to change someone who is self-destructive, to convince someone who doesn't love us to love us. As long as our well-being and self-worth are dependent on those around us, we are children hanging on our father's affection, waiting for our mothers to call us "darling," our teachers to tell us we are smart, our friends to include us in their clubs, we are waiting, waiting for enough kindness to break open the tight bud of our hearts.

❀✖❀

Marjorie is a participant in a Breaking Free workshop. She tells the group that she has been eating and throwing up for four years and three months.

I ask her what happened four years and three months ago.

She says, "I was raped by someone I knew."

"Would you like to tell us about it?" I ask.

She nods her head yes and then begins. "It was awful—I screamed and I started kicking and shoving him, biting him, but it didn't help, he was bigger and stronger than me and I gave up. Afterwards, I was bruised and banged up, but I didn't tell anyone. I didn't want anyone to know. Except my boyfriend, and he tried to take care of me but there was no way. I didn't want him to touch me. I was a virgin before the rape and I didn't want to have sex ever again. My boyfriend and I broke up and I started eating and throwing up. Five, six times a day. I would walk around in dangerous neighborhoods alone at night, eating and then throwing up in a garbage pail. I didn't care what happened to me. I thought the rape was my fault, that I shouldn't have let it happen, that I asked for it in some way, that I should have been able to fight back. I thought I was dirty, disgusting—used merchandise.

"When I was hospitalized because I tried to kill myself with an overdose of pills, I read your books. I realized that I was hovering between life and death and I realized I wanted to live. I've started therapy with a wonderful therapist—a man—and I've even stopped throwing up for weeks at a time; it's taken me so long to even begin to believe that what happened isn't my fault. I feel like I died and it's been tough coming back to life."

When she tells us about her childhood, she says that her father was an alcoholic. "Until the rape, I never looked at issues from my past. It was as if the rape was the catalyst and suddenly the immense amount of self-hatred I had been walking around with for my whole life came pouring out of me. I couldn't stand myself. The eating and throwing up was as disgusting a thing as I could do."

"You created something to hate yourself about," I say.

"I was so confused," she said. "I felt so violated. My dad had sexually abused me as a child and I never told anyone, but I felt as if that was my fault, too. Until the rape, I never mentioned it. I never even remembered it."

It was not her fault. Period. But the extent to which she heals the pain of her father's behavior, then of the rape, or kills herself slowly because of it, *is* in her hands, not in the rapist's.

When we have been violated—sexually, physically, or emotionally—the process of healing includes denial, confusion, rage, grief, and acceptance.* There is no right way to go through the stages of healing, nor is there any limit on how long each stage lasts. Feelings cannot be skipped; you get out of them by going through them.

If you are willing to go through each stage, to enter your feelings instead of wishing they would go away, if you have at least one person to whom you can tell the entire truth, someone who believes you, accepts you, loves you, you can surface on the other side of violation, abuse, and suffering, no matter how bad it was.

Some people don't heal. They get stuck in one of the stages. It is too frightening to acknowledge what really happened or to connect the feelings with the events.

My friend Poppie told me that she went to a therapist last month for an initial interview and the therapist told her she had a lot of grieving to do. Her father had abandoned her on the footsteps of the next-door neighbor's house when she was three, she hasn't seen her mother for thirty-five years, and although she has been in touch with her father for many years, she is forever furious with him. When she speaks of her father, she begins many sentences with: "After what he did to me . . . " When she forgets her father's birthdays, when she doesn't return her father's calls for weeks, when she tells her father she will meet him at six and doesn't show up until seven-thirty, she says, "After what my father did to me, he has no right to complain about what *I* do."

---

* See Elisabeth Kübler-Ross's stages of grieving in *On Death and Dying* (New York: Macmillan, 1969). While it is true that grieving for a life differs in many ways from grieving for the lost years, the stages of grief are similar, and the reader may find them helpful to know about.

Poppie doesn't want to hear about grieving. "When that therapist told me I had a lot of grieving to do, I said, "I'm looking forward, not backward.""

Poppie acknowledges her loss, tells stories about the neighbor named Josephine who gagged her with prunes and tied her hands behind her back. But her voice is as sucked of moisture as a piece of dry ice. While acknowledging the loss, she is denying the impact. She knows she is angry with her father, but her anger is a broken record that hasn't moved from its groove for thirty-five years. *After what my father did to me, after what my father did to me, after what my father did to me.* In trying to get back at her father for the injustice of childhood, Poppie forgets to notice what her anger is doing to herself.

Poppie got married last month. It is her third marriage, and she says she is very much in love with her new husband. She says she has never been happier. She says, "This is it, Geneen. This is the real one, the love I've been waiting for. What did that therapist know, anyway? Who says I have to look back?"

But the pain of her childhood has not gone anywhere; it is still locked inside her body, still imprinted on her cells. When her husband does something that evokes a constellation of painful memories, Poppie will unleash the anger of being gagged with prunes in a neighbor's home. When her husband leaves on a trip and doesn't return on schedule, she may feel like a three-year-old being abandoned by her father. Her husband will receive the pain, bewilderment, and fury of the child that Poppie refuses to make space for. He won't understand the depth of her pain. Neither will Poppie. Her feelings will be tremendously out of proportion to the events that trigger it. My guess is that it won't be long before I hear her talking bitterly about him. It won't be long before she puts herself to sleep with the refrain: *After what he did to me, after what he did to me, after what he did to me.*

❀✖❀

A friend of Matt's* says that couples enter a relationship madly in love, carrying a suitcase filled with clothes from past relationships, adolescence, childhood. By the time they have been together for a couple of years, they have removed all the clothes from their respective suitcases, thrown them on each other, and in utter disbelief exclaimed, "You aren't the person I fell in love with. I hardly recognize you."

We can't look forward without looking back.

We can't have healing relationships in the present without being willing to heal the pain of the past.

To heal, we have to believe that healing is possible. We must want to heal more than we are afraid to feel—rage, grief, sorrow. We must want to heal more than we want anything or anyone else.

❀✖❀

In the practice of insight meditation,† you learn to sit quietly and notice the feelings that repeat themselves. Worry, anxiety, fear. You notice fear and you label it: fear, fear. You notice what fear feels like in your body, how your stomach constricts, the tight ring around your heart, the tensions in your fingers, toes, face. And you don't stop. You breathe in, then out, and you keep noticing it: fear, fear. And if you pay very close attention, if you stay with the fear and don't push it away because it's uncomfortable to feel, you travel a layer deeper, you uncover what you are afraid of: not being loved, being separate. And you keep noticing and you keep breathing. When you are present with the root of your fear, you stop being afraid. You are breathing in and out, you are not pushing anything away, you are fully in

---

* Thank you, Annette Goodheart.

† For a guide to insight meditation, see *Seeking the Heart of Wisdom*, by Joseph Goldstein and Jack Kornfield (Boston: Shambhala, 1987).

the moment. The act of being fully in the moment, alive to the subtleties of sensation, feeling, awake to color, sound, temperature, the awareness of life as it is—not as it was, not as it could have been, not as you wish it would be—is what being alive is about.

❀✖❀

During the days after the conversation with Dick in the lobby of the Claremont Hotel, I felt like a piece of bruised meat. And I blamed him for it. My mind was an endless loop of things I wished I had said: I should have told him that he had some nerve to tell me about the Ten Commandments, I should have told him that he had to talk to me at the table or not at all, I should have used his life as an example of everything he was telling me not to do, I should have protected myself.

The incident triggered an onslaught of childhood memories in which I felt hurt and trapped and unable to fight back. Dick became all the people in my life from whom I could not protect myself or had not protected myself. It didn't matter that in the conversation with him I *had* protected myself. I believed that my pain was his fault and I wanted to hurt him back. I believed that making him feel bad would make me feel good. I could feel powerful if he would be powerless. I became the quintessential victim.

I wrote a letter to Dick in which I expressed my anger. When I finished reading the letter to Matt, I said, "That's all," and he said, "That's enough."

"Can't you say anything else?"

Silence. I should have known not to read this to him. He's such a goody-goody, always trying to "communicate," always trying to smooth things out, not ruffle any feathers, not get engaged in conflict.

Matt said, "Perhaps you should examine your motives for sending this letter. If what you want is to fight with Dick and widen the distance that is already there, mail it. But if I was him, I would be so busy defending myself from your attack that I wouldn't listen to the truth of what you were saying."

"So what am I supposed to do, turn the other cheek? I'm not righteous; I'm furious. I think he was a real shit and I want to tell him that."

"What he did wasn't so awful. The guy doesn't know any better; he was trying to protect your mother. It was only awful because it reminded you of your past. You're in pain because of what was done to you twenty years ago—Dick had no part in that."

He's right. I hate it when he's right, especially when I am so attached to doing something that I see I shouldn't do. I want to send this letter. I want revenge. If he hurts more, then I will hurt less.

Matt's gaze is steady. "What are you thinking about?" he asks.

"Revenge," I answer.

"Ah," he says, smiling so that the space between his two front teeth shows, "the conscious person's way of dealing with pain."

"Exactly," I say, feeling a crack in the cement wall of my chest for the first time in days.

❧✖❧

I raged for a week. I struggled in therapy to examine the old and familiar feelings that Dick had triggered. I meditated in the mornings and watched the rage bubble to the front of my mind; I labeled it "rage, rage." I talked to Matt about it, to Sara about it, I wrote in my journal, wrote three letters to Dick that I never sent.

By the time I wrote—and sent—the fourth letter, the rage had turned to sadness, the sadness to acceptance and openness. The letter was clear and without anger: it described my reasons for writing the book and the fact that its publication was not negotiable. It also expressed my desire to let go of the past and to have a loving relationship with my mother.

The next time I saw Dick, he said, "I reread the Molly piece in *Feeding the Hungry Heart*. I sat in the den and read it over and over. I cried. I couldn't stop crying. I haven't read it since the book came out seven years ago. I couldn't stand to feel your pain, Geneen. If I read your words, then I have to feel your pain, and I'm afraid to feel it. I can't stand to think of you suffering so much. It hurts too much. And I'm afraid that I'll get angry at Ruth. Will you forgive me for acting like a jerk?"

I am fortunate to have Dick in my life. It is unusual for a parent to be willing to examine himself or herself with such honesty. He considers what I say and allows my thoughts and feelings to have an effect on his actions. He isn't afraid to admit he's made a mistake. But by the time he apologized, I didn't need him to apologize.

I had spoken the truth as I saw it and did not betray myself.

I had relinquished responsibility for my mother's well-being and stopped protecting her from wounds she helped to create. In letting go of blaming myself for her pain, I had stopped blaming her for mine.

I had cycled through the seasons of my sorrow and emerged with a quiet heart. A quiet heart is all I wanted to begin with. Or end with.

CHAPTER

8

Being Strong

in the

Broken Places

When we lived on Eightieth Street in Jackson Heights, a woman named Bette Davis lived across the street from us in a small, mysterious apartment. The curtains were green velvet with black fringes and the floor was a carpet of peonies. I made up any excuse to visit Bette; I thought she was exotic because her name was the same as a movie star's and because she had a beauty mark on her right cheek and because her hair smelled like rose water. I loved sitting in the rocking chair next to her, asking questions about her life while she crocheted squares of a black-and-yellow afghan. Where was she born, did she want to get married, what did she do at her job. Bette was twenty-six, worked as a stewardess for Eastern Airlines and I wanted her to be my mother.

After I left her apartment and returned to my mother's house, I'd daydream about what my life would be like if Bette were my mother: She wouldn't yell at me. I'd have a beauty mark on my right cheek. Life would smell like summer.

When I became a ballerina in a baby-blue leotard with a rainbow-colored tutu, I wanted Sandy, my dance teacher, to be my mother. I practiced walking like a duck so that I would walk like her and I curled long pieces of hair in front of my ears so that my hair would look like her daughter Chloe's hair. When she invited me for dinner and served ham with pineapple, I held my nose and ate it even though I had never eaten ham before and was worried that God would punish me. I wanted her to call me darling and read *The Island of the Blue Dolphins* to me at bedtime.

When John Kennedy was shot, I wanted Jackie to be my mother. I wanted to be famous like Caroline and John-John and I wanted to be brave in the face of tragedy.

In high school, I wanted my boyfriend Ray's mother to be my mother; she set a place for me at dinner every night, asked me about my homework, and stocked her refrigerator with Cool-Whip and strawberries, which were my daily staples.

I bought Jil's mother scented candles in the shape of leprechauns because she was beautiful and collected candles and I wanted her to love me.

Mark's mother made me butter cookies and wrote me letters at college. She told me I was smart and she was proud of me.

I turned to Nona's mother for advice about boys and birth control.

Every time I made a new friend, I wanted to belong to her family. I wanted to be part of a brood of children with a mother and father who ate dinner together and spent Sundays at the Museum of Natural History and made campfires at Lake George in the summer. I wanted to be on the inside of the glow of a loving family. I wanted to be almost anyone but myself with almost any family but my own.

❧✖❧

For one year, between the ages of twelve and thirteen, I went to Temple Beth-El Sunday school. Mrs. Bernstein taught us about Moses and Jacob and Ruth and Naomi, about Pharaoh and killing the firstborn, eating unleavened bread on Passover, blowing the shofar at Rosh Hashanah. Rabbi Weissman told us stories as we sat in the temple on long wooden benches with prayerbooks stuck in blue velvet pockets: "Once upon a time, a long, long time ago, a rabbi took the people in his village to a big tree a mile away. He told them that this was the Trouble Tree and that they could hang their troubles on it. All the people unrolled their troubles from their bags. Some people's troubles were stuck to long strips of red-and-white cloth; those with little troubles sewed theirs to tiny squares of blue silk. It took a long time for the villagers to hang up their troubles, and for a while, it looked as though there were too many troubles and not enough branches, but finally all the bags were empty and the tree looked like a liquid rainbow, it had so many colors on it, all swaying in the breeze. The people of the village spent the day playing together, singing songs, eating a meal, and talking. At the end of the day, the rabbi said, "We must go home now. Each of you must take a trouble from the tree. You can take the one you brought with you or you can take another person's trouble. Whose trouble will you choose?"

At this point in the story, I was thinking that if it were me and Glenna were there, I would take her troubles because she had a mother and a father who were home every night and who took her places on Saturday afternoons. Or I would take Randy's troubles because she didn't look as if she *had* any; hers was probably sewn on a piece of blue silk that was so tiny it blew away.

". . . and what do you think the people did?" the rabbi asked.

Ronald Smith said, "I bet it was a big mess because no one could decide which trouble to take or else everyone wanted the same person's trouble."

"No," the rabbi said. "Everyone wanted the same trouble they brought with them. No one wanted to switch."

I would have switched, I thought. I definitely would have switched. Anyone's life but mine, anyone's family but my own. I believed that my trouble was the only *real* trouble and that having anyone else's would be no trouble at all.

I've changed my mind.

Hemingway says that the world breaks everyone and some of

us are strong in the broken places. The purpose of healing is to be strong in the broken places.

As a child, I created a world of my own because the world I was living in was not home to me. I wrote stories about planets with purple rings, poems about feathers and hummingbirds. I wrote my first book when I was twelve. I became a writer.

As a child, I learned to hear the unspoken, to climb behind my mother's face, my father's eyes. I learned to see where others only looked. I became a teacher.

I learned that nothing was as it seemed. I learned that money didn't make anyone happy. I learned about death and violence, cheating, lying, stealing, and I learned about humor, determination, endurance. I broke into ten thousand pieces. Who I am today is a result of the way in which I put the pieces together.

When I first knew that there was a way out of compulsive eating besides dieting, I put an ad in the paper that read: "Compulsive eating support group for women. I think it's possible to stop dieting and lose weight and I think it's possible to learn how to nourish ourselves in ways besides food and I think it's possible to find out why we use food. If you would like to participate in these discoveries, call Geneen at 425-1185. The cost is $1 a night for ten weeks."

Ten women called and enrolled for the group. Since I didn't have a place to live, I asked my friends Sue and Harry if I could hold the first group at their house, which was on a country road in Aptos. For their convenience and because the house was hard to find, I told the women that I would meet them in front of Jay's Liquor in the Aptos village shopping center and we would caravan to Harry and Sue's living room.

I was forty pounds over my natural weight and I wanted to look presentable for the first session, so I decided to get an air-dry permanent two days before the first meeting. I had to sleep on the rollers for two nights because my hair is thin and permanents don't take well, and when I went back to the salon on the afternoon before the first group, I was told that the hairdresser had had to get an emergency operation and I would have to sleep on the rollers one more night.

I waved to ten women I didn't know in front of Jay's Liquor and told them I was their leader. "It's me," I said, "I'm the leader of the group." I stood there shivering in the November night, forty pounds over my natural weight with rollers in my hair. One woman's jaw dropped open. Another woman said, "Thank you very much. I'm going home."

The years I spent dieting and bingeing were living hell, but the path I followed as I realized compulsive eating was my friend taught me to believe in myself, to laugh at myself, to have courage, to take risks, to enter life more deeply than I ever thought possible. I've used the pain of compulsion as a way into the unspeakable in me; it's given me compassion for others who struggle with food; it's provided me with a system to understand trust, fear, nourishment, and satisfaction. The weakest places in me as a child are some of the strongest places in me as an adult. They are strong now because—not in spite of—being weak then.

It's not the wound that determines the quality of your life, it's what you do with the wound—how you hold it, carry it, dance with it, or bury yourself under it.

No one knows where dreams are born. And what gives people the grit to follow them. Lucille Ball's father died when she was four. Her mother remarried but sent Lucille to live with relatives. They put a dog collar around her neck and tied her to a tree in the back yard to keep her from wandering. While her body was tied down, her mind wandered. She created a friend called Sassafras, who comforted her and told her she would be a famous movie star.

Life is what happens as you live with the wounds. Life is not a matter of getting the wounds out of the way so that you can finally live. Wounds are never permanently erased. We are fragile beings, and some days we break all over again

In January of last year, Matt and I flew into Phoenix. While he was waiting for the luggage to arrive, I walked over to the American Airlines desk to purchase a ticket for another trip. The line was long; I waited for half an hour. Matt and I had not been specific about who would meet whom and where we would meet. After my business was done, I began waiting for Matt to show up. Fifteen minutes passed, twenty, thirty minutes. This was the story I told myself: "He forgot about me. He left the airport. I don't know the name of the hotel we are staying in, or even the city. Maybe it's not Phoenix, maybe it's Scottsdale. No problem. I'll just take a cab to an airport hotel, keep calling my answering machine to see if he calls, and we'll connect sometime this evening. If we don't, it doesn't matter, I'm flying out tomorrow anyway." Doesn't matter? My heart was racing. I was bewildered that Matt had left without looking for me, but I did what I had done as a child: I figured out how to care for myself and pretended none of it mattered. That decided, it occurred to me to page him on the white courtesy phone as a last effort to find him. He showed up at the American Airlines desk within three minutes.

"I thought you forgot about me and left the airport."

"You what?"

"I thought you forgot about me."

"You're kidding, aren't you? I live with you, sleep with you, talk to you every day of my life—and I am schlepping thirteen pieces of your luggage. *How could I forget about you?* I've been waiting for you by the luggage counter for an hour and fifteen minutes."

"Oh."

I am an abandonment person. Three years ago, I stopped talking to Matt when he was about to leave on a trip. Then we created a "going-away" ritual in which we sat with each other for a half hour on the day before he left and talked about our feelings. Mine were always the same: I told him that if he loved me, he wouldn't leave me, and that if he was leaving me, he couldn't love me, and if he didn't love me, I didn't want to make myself vulnerable and love him. He told me that he wasn't my mother or my father, he told me that he was coming back in two days, he told me he loved me. The ritual worked for about a year. Then my fears caved in and I started creating distance when he returned.

Wounds are never permanently erased. Being an abandonment person changes from year to year, depending on how conscious I am about that piece of myself. How much I am willing to risk, how patient I am willing to be, how much mercy I can give to the part of me that is forever frightened of being left. The way I work with my fear of abandonment shapes the curves and colors of my life the way a river shapes a canyon wall.

Healing is about opening our hearts, not closing them. It is about softening the places in us that won't let love in. Healing is a process. It is about rocking back and forth between the abuse of the past and the fullness of the present and being in the present more and more of the time. It is rocking that creates the healing, not staying in one place or another. The purpose of healing is not to be forever happy; that is impossible. The purpose of healing is to be awake. And to live while you are alive instead of dying while you are alive. Healing is about being broken and whole at the same time.

❧✖❧

When we realize, as a one- or three- or ten-year-old, that we are too vulnerable for the world in which we find ourselves, we plaster our bodies with protective casts and we draw pretty pictures and we write our names and we let other people draw pictures and write their names, and by the time we are grown-ups, every single inch of the cast is jammed with color and we've gotten so used to the feel of it and so attached to the drawings we've made that we forget that our bodies are underneath.

When we realize how painful this cast is, weighing our bones down and restricting our movements, when we realize we've outgrown this childhood form and don't need it any more, the task of sawing it away seems so immense and so painful that we don't know whether we should bother. Especially when we notice that almost all the people we know or see are walking around in their cast. And everyone is so busy admiring, even envying someone else's cast that we wonder if we are imagining things. Maybe this really is my skin, we say to ourselves. How could they all be so happy with their bodies covered in plaster? And we feel as lonely as we did in childhood.

Compulsive eating is the cast, not the wound, although most people don't believe that.

❧✖❧

Five years ago, I received a phone call from Karen Russell, a woman in Vancouver, British Columbia, who wanted to attend a workshop that I was leading in Santa Cruz. When I asked her to tell me about herself, she said that she had read *Breaking Free* and was very moved by it. "I weigh 420 pounds," she said. The workshop was already filled, but I told her I would call her if there was a cancellation.

When I hung up the phone, I called Sara, who was leading the workshop with me, and told her about Karen's call.

Sara said, "Have you ever worked with someone who weighed over 300 pounds?"

"No."

"What does 420 pounds look like?" Sara asked.

"I don't know," I answered. "And I'm concerned about her comfort—whether she can fit on a chair—and how high her expectations will be. It's a long way to travel for a two-day workshop. Maybe I should refer her to someone in Vancouver."

Two days later, we received a cancellation for the workshop. I called Karen and talked with her about my considerations. She said she wanted to come, would I please consider the possibility? Fine, I said. I'll see you on Saturday in Santa Cruz.

This is her story:

By the time I was thirty-seven, I weighed 424 pounds according to the freight scale at Johnson's Trucking Terminal. I couldn't buy clothes even in large-size women's specialty shops because their sizes stopped at 52 and I was a size 60. My wardrobe consisted of three caftans which I had had specially made: one each—navy, black, and brown—sewn straight up the sides with openings for my head and arms. I wore slip-on sandals in summer and winter because I couldn't bend over to lace sneakers up and dress shoes buckled under my weight. I didn't own a coat, but that didn't matter since I was hardly ever out of the house anyway. In the morning, I'd maneuver myself out of bed, go to the kitchen, get my stash of food, and settle into my chair in the living room, comforted by the assurance that food was all around me. My days were filled with the drone of soap operas in the background. I lived my life vicariously through my husband and children. They became my arms and legs and my window to the outside world. When I went anywhere, I drove. The car became part of my insulation, my armor, my protection. I used to drive around town eating, stuffing down anger, guilt, hurt—eating until nothing mattered any more.

Chip, my fifteen-year-old, plays baseball. Every ball season for eight years, I drove to the park to watch him play. I didn't miss many of his games, either, but I watched them all from the safe insulation of the car. I was always meticulously careful about where I parked: close enough to see the game but camouflaged enough so that the other kids or their parents couldn't see me. I wanted to be out there, on the bleachers behind home plate, but I couldn't risk embarrassing Chip or suffering the humiliation and rejection I knew would be imminent if I cracked the car door open even a little bit. I'd get as comfortable as I could and watch the game with my stash of pizza, soda pop, and Oreos to keep me company.

I tried to break free from my state of nonexistence hundreds of times. I'd been to scores of doctors. "Exercise, dear," they'd say. "Just *push* yourself away from the table three times a day." I went to a weight-loss organization where a lady was given pig ears to wear during the meeting because she'd been "bad" that week and gained two pounds. Another organization applauded if you'd been "good," and an uncomfortable silence settled on all of those who hadn't lost weight that week. I never went back to either group. I tried countless others as well, but the messages I received were all the same: "You're weak, undisciplined, lazy . . . you have tarnished character and questionable integrity . . . you're not very bright . . . you can't trust yourself . . . here are the rules. Trust *us*. We know what is best for you. Don't step outside these lines." I tried and failed so many times that I felt shell-shocked and battle-fatigued and I only wanted it all to stop.

One morning, as I was sitting in my chair, "Donahue" came on. Three guests were talking about weight-related issues and I was intrigued. During that program, from the very coldest part of my numbness, I felt some warmth. Geneen spoke in a dialect my heart knew well; I was deeply moved that someone understood where I was . . . and was speaking about it on national TV with compassion and eloquence.

After the show, I phoned the bookstores in town and located a copy of *Breaking Free*. I read and cried then read and cried some more. I called Geneen's office; two weeks later I left Vancouver on a Greyhound bus headed for San Francisco.

One of the most poignant concepts that I was able to experience in the workshop was that there is no failure—no right or wrong—in this process. I had been looking at my conflicts with food in a rigid linear way when in fact they are more like a spiral. Like jumping out of a plane, pulling the rip cord, discovering there's no parachute—but then discovering there's no ground. It's a going-deeper process, and I realized I wanted to be awake and alive for all of it. I decided to replace judgment with awareness as often as I could. Instead of saying, "You've blown it, stupid . . . you'll never get it right," I would say to myself, "Okay, you're eating when you're not hungry—what's going on?"

In the past whenever something hurt too much, I would pack up and leave myself because I was afraid that if I experienced the fear, it would eat me alive. I made a commitment to stay with myself, let the fear or hurt wash over me.

Three and half years later, I'm still in the breaking-free process. This journey has taken me to some breathless places and I live in awareness much more of the time than I ever dreamed I could.

I've lost 275 pounds. Last spring, I bought my first ever pair of jeans and sweatshirts and sweaters and sneakers and blouses. I work at a job in which I feel fulfilled with people who are becoming my friends. I park the car now and hike in the lush woods along the Cowichan River. I came out of the car and onto the bleachers. I am the team mother for Chip's all-star team and the secretary of the Baseball Association. Now I love colorful, flamboyant clothes—and roller coasters. There have been rough times, too. Some things have surfaced that I need help in working through and I've begun therapy. The reality is that some weeks therapy is painful. I'm finding more and more though that if I can unclench and soften instead of steeling myself against it, the pain changes color and intensity and I don't have to eat to make it bearable.

❧✕❧

I spent a day with Karen recently. I wanted to know what made the difference. I wanted to know why, after thirty-seven years of trying to lose weight and feeling like a failure, she could come to a two-day workshop and spend the next three and a half years practicing what she learned there. I wanted to know why, at 420 pounds, she was not overcome with fear during the first month of eating what she wanted when she saw that she was gaining, not losing weight.

She said, "I was waking up every morning with pains in my chest. I couldn't walk more than half a block without getting winded and needing to turn around. I didn't want to kill myself, but I wanted someone to take me silently. When I saw you on TV, it was as if I realized that I had been exiled from my homeland and someone was talking my language, telling me I could go home again. When I read your book, I cried for the first time in twenty years. I was dying, Geneen. There was no other choice for me."

My friend Maria, who also works with compulsive eaters by teaching them to legalize food and stop dieting, says that Karen must have had a core of ego strength that enabled her to follow through with what she learned at the weekend workshop. She says she must have had a person who loved her as a child, maybe a babysitter. Someone who taught her that she was lovable, someone who gave her the strength and resolve to take care of herself. I ask Karen about this. She says it wasn't early love; it was having no choice. It was knowing she was dying.

The first step in change for a compulsive eater is acknowledging the desperation—realizing that the choices they make on a daily level are about living or dying—and making the choice to live.

We become compulsive about food because we have something to hide. Something we believe is worse than being fat or eating compulsively. The process of breaking free from compulsive eating is one of keeping steady with food so that we can discover what we are hiding. But until we believe that compulsive eating means something, until we stop shrugging it off as an acceptable obsession that can be fixed with will power, a protein shake, or the cut of a surgeon's knife, until we realize that compulsion is the cast, not the wound, until we realize we are dying, we will not have the information we need to decide to live.

Alcoholics and drug addicts visibly lose their lives to their addictions; they smash up their cars, track their arms with needles. Compulsive eaters don't know how to recognize bottom because their lives are rarely messy. They pick up their children from school after bingeing all day, they go to work after purging three times in the morning, they take care of friends, spouses, people who need them. Their speech is not slurred, their motor coordination is not impaired; they are dependable, wise, responsive. Alcoholics go out with a bang; those who hit bottom and are fortunate enough to know it have a chance to come back up. Compulsive eaters drown when no one is looking because they don't want to bother anyone.

I spoke with a woman named Rachel yesterday on the telephone. She's been following the eating guidelines* for two years, and although she's pleased she hasn't gained any weight, she wants to lose weight. I asked her if what she said was true—that she follows the guidelines.

"Do you only eat when you are hungry and do you stop when you've had enough?"

"No," she said.

"Why not?"

"I'm scared of what would happen if I lost weight. Who knows how my relationships would change, or my job? I have been to so many kinds of weight loss programs, and whenever they get hard, I don't want to do the work. Then I start thinking that the program doesn't work. Then I go on to the next one."

An alcoholic who smashes her car and gets arrested for driving while intoxicated doesn't have the luxury of rambling to the next program. Her addiction backs her into a corner where court appearances and shattered relationships follow her like a trail of dried blood until she has to do something about it and them— or die.

Compulsive eaters have no apparent urgency to provoke or inspire them. They don't choose between life and death; they choose between eating ice cream or drinking a liquid protein shake. Or so it appears.

---

* See *Why Weight: A Guide to Ending Compulsive Eating* (New York: Plume, 1989) for an explanation of the eating guidelines.

And while the consequences of being ten or thirty pounds overweight are not the same as driving while intoxicated, compulsive eaters die a little every time they eat compulsively. The choice is exactly the same for all of us—alcoholics, drug addicts, cigarette smokers, compulsive eaters: Do I want to live while I'm alive and embrace what sustains me or do I want to die while I'm alive and embrace what destroys me? If I choose life, where do I need to heal? What are my secrets? What pieces of me have I been unwilling to recognize? What images, what nightmares, what words am I most afraid to speak?

⊛✖⊛

Karen's father suffered a nervous breakdown when she was twelve; her mother committed him to a mental institution. One day she returned from school and he was gone. No letters, no phone calls. Karen never saw him again. She started to overeat. "When I was lonely, food was my best friend. When I missed my dad, food comforted me. When I was angry, food calmed me. My mother was working four to midnight and when I'd come home after school to an empty house, she'd phone from work and tell me what was in the refrigerator. Nothing hurt so much that it couldn't be obliterated with food. I made it through the next twenty-four years of my life by engaging automatic pilot. I went to the university, got married, had children—but experienced very little of it."

She married a man who was twenty-one years older than she. "I married my dad," she says. Indeed. She was a twelve-year-old child aching to live with her dad. She was a twelve-year-old who was taught that her feelings were too big for the world in which she lived. Her mother and her Aunt Emily and her Uncle Bernie never asked how she felt about her father going away, never made room for sadness or loneliness, so she entombed the feelings in 420 pounds of flesh.

When she meets me at the airport, Karen is wearing a paisley scarf slung over her shoulder and jeans with a wide red belt. Her hair is in a ponytail. She looks fifteen years old and I tell her so. "I *am* fifteen years old," she says. "When I first lost weight, I went back to being twelve because that's the age at which I began gaining weight and burying myself underground. But I've progressed in the past few years," she says, grinning. "Soon I'll be sixteen and ready to date."

Karen notices everything—sounds, smells, textures. And she giggles a lot, a high, wild giggle. I find myself wishing that I could see the world as she sees the world, with a beginner's mind. She swings back and forth between an irrepressible and unself-conscious joy and speaking solemnly but evenly about the painful discoveries she is making in her life. At one point she says, "Geneen, put your hands here. I have to show you something." She takes my hands and puts them on her hips. "I have hip bones. I actually have hip bones. Can you believe that?"

Later she tells me, "I was twenty years old and had never been on a date. I was teaching in a Baptist school, and one day a kid in my class was reading the *Globe* during an English exam. I took it away from him and read it myself. People had put personal ads in there, looking for dates and all kinds of kinky things. My girlfriend dared me to put an ad of my own in there, and I took her up on the dare. I got forty replies, and one of them seemed as if it was from a nice guy. We corresponded for six months, then starting talking to each other on the phone. One day, he asked me to marry him."

"Without having met you?" I asked.

"Without having met me," she replied. "And I said yes, without having met him. I told him I weighed 380 pounds, but he didn't seem to care. He flew into Indianapolis on Friday night, we got the blood tests on Monday, and Tuesday, we were married. On Wednesday, we drove to Vancouver and moved in with his mother."

I gasp, horrified at the thought of agreeing to marry someone I'd never met. *And moving in with his mother.*

Karen is laughing. "Pretty amazing, isn't it? But I needed a way out of my dry, horrible life and Dan offered it to me. The problem was that there wasn't any love between us. There still isn't. Dan is fine as long as I leave him alone. When I weighed 420 pounds, it was enough to have a husband who didn't drink or beat me. But it's not enough any more. I haven't been touched for ten years. I want to live a loving life, even if it means living alone. It's too painful."

"Losing weight brings you a different kind of pain, doesn't it?"

She nods her head yes. "When I weighed 420 pounds, I was dying from the pain of numbness. Now I am living. It's the difference between eating my feelings and feeling my feelings."

"Would you ever go back?"

"Are you kidding? My doctor told me a few months ago that I was manic depressive. He said I was feeling too much and swinging from sadness to joy too easily. He gave me drugs to take. I went home and thought about what he said—and I got very angry. I went back to him and said, "Look, I spent thirty-seven years of my life eating away my feelings, and now that I'm not using food, it makes perfect sense that all those feelings are coming up, but I'm glad they are. If you can't handle them, I'll find a doctor who can.""

We are sitting across the room from each other on a pair of white couches. Karen says, "It's not just the loveless marriage, it was my loveless childhood. My mother was mean and bossy. Her idea of a Sunday afternoon was picking the lint off the curtains. I hated her for driving my father away. But it's recently occurred to me that he abandoned me. He got out of the mental institution in six months and never called me, never tried to see me. I'm just now letting myself feel the sadness and anger of those years."

Compulsive eating is the cast, not the wound. Losing the fat brings her face to face with the wounds that created it.

But it's not the wound that shapes our lives, it's the choice we make as adults between embracing our wounds or raging against them.

The second step in change for a compulsive eater is learning how to be infinitely tender with every single part of you that you detest—including your fat. This step is the work of a lifetime.

When Karen Russell came to the workshop, she said, "It was the first time in my life that anyone told me I was not bad, I was not worthless, that I deserved kindness and compassion.

"I grew up to believe in an angry God," she says, "a God who punishes you, a God who is never pleased, for whom only perfection is enough. I went from an angry mother to an angry God to being angry at myself. Diets were an extension of the angry God; I could never be good enough. I would always rebel and feel horrible about myself afterwards. At the workshop, I realized that I was not bad and that openheartedness, not punishment, was the way into my problems with food. The fist in the middle of my chest opened for the first time in my life."

The difference between Karen Russell and hundreds of thousands of people who are struggling with their weight or any other addiction is that Karen began, as she calls it, "sitting with herself" when she binged instead of turning against herself. She began using overeating as a way to gain access to her feelings instead of as proof that she was worthless and would never get it right. It was as if she had been an outsider to her own life, sitting in merciless judgment of herself, and now she was going to let herself into her heart. It is the difference between kicking a child who is in pain or rocking her.

Most people kick because they've been kicked and they don't know how to do anything else. They feel that being kind to themselves, using their pain as a guide, is self-indulgent and cannot possibly lead to change.

Most people rage against their eating. They hate it and themselves. They're tired of spending so much time thinking about their obsession with food. They want to be done, but their impatience to end their misery prolongs it. Hate does not heal anyone, ever.

Karen shows me the flab hanging under her chin and arms. She says, "My therapist gave me the name of a plastic surgeon. He wants to do a tummy tuck, cut off the excess skin from my bottom ribs to my pubic area, from hip to hip. He'd have to make me a new navel. Then a breast reduction . . . then my upper arms . . . then my thighs. I don't know how I feel about this. I'm into bones and flab these days. I like my bones. They're big and strong, solid and grounding. My flab is part of me, too. It's my battle scar. I don't want to cut it away just yet; I feel very kindly towards it."

❧✖❧

I received this letter from Karen last week:

A few weeks ago someone I love ran their fingers lightly through my hair and kissed my forehead. It was a bittersweet feeling because it flooded me with wonder, and at the same time, the lack of love in my life glared at me in stark neon. Despite what I've been through in my process with food, I ended up at the grocery store after work. I spent forty-five minutes wandering up and down the aisles. I stopped at the bakery department and picked up some croissants, held them tenderly, smelled their soft, yeasty aroma. Tears welled up in my eyes and I placed them gently back on the shelf. Next, I hit the rice section: Quaker's Savory Spring Vegetable and Cheese. I shook the box and it responded with a dull thud. Again the tears came and again I put the food back. Next I found myself embracing (yes, actually embracing) a large jar of Miracle Whip. It felt cold and glassy and I realized that nothing in that store could satisfy me. I hungered for something that couldn't be bought there—or anywhere. So I left the store with nothing. And with everything: my sense of self was intact.

Trevor is a fourteen-year-old boy. I met him at baseball registration last month. He stood in front of me, a big awkward kid, nervously fingering the brim of an old ball cap. He stuttered: "I . . . I . . . I just want to play ball." He told me that when he was a little boy, a wild hard pitch drilled him in the face and he had not been able to play ball since that day. But now, at an age when lots of boys quit, Trevor was ready to start.

I feel like Trevor, standing on the brink of a new ball season, just starting a game at fourteen that most boys have played since they were six. Nervously fingering the brim of an old ball cap and saying, "Hey! I want to play so bad I can taste it. Can I?" It seems like the team rosters are already made up and maybe there won't be space for a forty-two-year-old coming so late to the game.

But I'm ALIVE and I feel everything with great vibrancy. I walk in the woods and feel a hushed sense of awe. Driving around in the warm spring rain a few weeks ago, I was spellbound by a double rainbow. Last month, I went on an arduous hike. When I came down the mountainside, an elderly English woman walked over to meet me and invited me to her place because there was something she wanted to show me. As we walked into her greenhouse, the smell of over one hundred fifty orchids in different stages of growth and bloom mingled to the point of intoxication. Crimson reds, creamy whites, outrageous purples from Guatemala and Costa Rica. Last week at work, I looked out the window and saw some bare oak trees covered with raindrops. I knew they were just raindrops on a naked tree, but to me they were diamonds.

I wish I could tell you that being a size twelve is all wonderful but I'm finding out that being awake and alive is a package deal. I don't get to go through the line and pick only goodies. On one side is wonder, awe, excitement and laughter—and on the other side is tears, disappointment, aching sadness. Wholeness is coming to me by being willing to explore ALL the feelings.

So . . . 275 pounds later, my life is a mixture of pain and bliss. It hurts a lot these days, but it's real. It's my life being lived by me and not vicariously through a soap opera the way it used to be. I don't know where all of this is leading, but one thing I know for sure: I'm definitely going.

Yes to the process instead of the goal. Yes to the wonder, yes to the sadness.
Yes. Yes.

CHAPTER

9

When Love Is Love

Sunday morning in Santa Barbara, ten years ago. I'm sitting with my friend Jil, whom I haven't seen for three years. The table is set with whole-wheat bagels and lox, cream cheese with scallions; there is fresh orange juice in porcelain mugs. We are talking about getting what you want in a relationship. Jil says I should make a list of the qualities I want in a man, that if I don't have a definite idea about the things I want, I can't expect to find them.

She smears her second bagel with cream cheese. "They really could have been more generous with the scallions," she says, turning to me. "You look pensive. What are you thinking about?"

"Sheldon," I answer. "I haven't thought about him for a long time. And my father. He couldn't come to the funeral, had a busy day at the office, told me that 'these things happen.' I felt as if Sheldon's death had set my bones on fire, and when my dad told me he couldn't go because he had a busy day at the office, I felt sorry for him and said I understood."

"Women get a crumb from their fathers," Jil said, "so when they get two crumbs from a man, they accept it."

Nick was my lover at the time of my meeting with Jil. Brainy, generous, married Nick. His wife knew about me and about his lover before me. She tolerated his affairs because she didn't like sex and this way she avoided it. The week before my visit with

Jil, Nick and I had a fight as he was leaving to pick up his daughter from school. I was angry that our meetings were sandwiched between his work at the office and his daughter's ballet lessons. When he walked in my door he'd kiss me passionately and tell me how beautiful I was. Then we'd walk to the bedroom and make love. Then our time would be up. I screamed at him: I am the dessert in your life, the chocolate. You come to me for the sweetness, but your main meal is your wife, your family. I want to be someone's main meal.

When, a week later, the women in my Breaking Free group brought their favorite food to the meeting, they all, every single one of the twelve, brought chocolate in some form. Cookies, candy, ice cream. After each person described the food she brought and why it was her favorite, how she felt when she ate it, the consensus was that although everyone loved the first bite, chocolate was an extra. It didn't sustain them. How do you feel when you eat this? I asked. Always sick and always empty, one woman answered.

Many of the women said they associated eating sweets with being with their fathers, with the way they were treated by their fathers. Underneath the liquid cherry-filled nights were mad cravings for mashed potatoes, rice and vegetables, whole-grain muffins. The sweets didn't satisfy them; they needed something more substantial.

❃✖❃

Compulsion does not develop in a vacuum; it begins in relationship. Compulsion is what we resorted to when we felt we didn't matter to people who mattered to us.

When I was in high school, I looked at thin girls who had acne or frizzy hair and thought, If I had your body or if you had my skin and straight hair, at least one of us would be pretty. I thought that the only thing wrong with me was that I was fat and if, by some miracle (for which I prayed every single day), I could wake up thin, I would be stunning and happy for the rest of my life. When relationships didn't work out, I shrugged them off to bad luck or to the fact that I was fat and that no one worth having would have me.

It didn't occur to me until two years before I met Matt that just as I ate compulsively for good reasons, I chose inappropriate partners for good reasons as well. The way I ate and the way I loved stemmed from the same source: the models of love I absorbed from my parents, and the self-image I constructed based on that love.

For seventeen years, I ate compulsively. For twenty-one years, I involved myself in relationships that left me feeling the same as eating compulsively: always sick and always empty. I had no idea how to take care of myself either with food or with people. Making myself sick from eating too much chocolate was no different from choosing partners for whom I could never be more than icing on the cake of their lives.

I didn't know that eating a meal was an act of kindness and would give my body the fuel it needed to think clearly, move fluidly. I thought it was naughty and therefore exciting to eat sugar-coated donuts for breakfast. I didn't know that choosing a kind, available partner was an act of kindness. I thought it was naughty and exciting to choose partners for whom I had to live on the edge of myself, balancing disaster with passion. Lovers with whom I could not rest.

I ate to shove my feelings away. I ate to make myself disappear. I didn't know that I was worth anything. And if I didn't know, I certainly couldn't pick lovers who did.

❧✖❧

Mike Goldman's arms and legs looked too long for his 6′3″ frame; he wasn't sure where to put them, what to do with them. But his mouth was soft and generous and I liked him immediately. I met him on the second day of freshman orientation and three weeks later I was dizzy in love. Mike was a senior at Tulane; he had a car, an apartment, a sense of humor. But Mike had one very large and unforgivable flaw: he loved me. He was interested in me, respected me, wanted what was best for me. And I couldn't stand it. I picked on him, didn't like the dandruff that littered his shirts, thought he looked ridiculous when he got his hair cut. After we had been dating for seven months, he asked me to marry him. I lied and said I would think about it. But I already knew the answer. Anyone who was stupid enough to love me, anyone for whom I didn't have to turn cartwheels and break my heart, was not someone I wanted to marry. The answer was no.

Two years after I broke up with him, a friend told me that Mike was getting married. The wedding was to be held at a temple in New Haven, Connecticut. I was in New York at the time, visiting my parents. I called Mike's mother and pretended to be Lillian Gillman from his class at Tulane. I said I was in town and heard that he was getting married and although I wasn't invited to the reception, I wondered whether I could come to the ceremony—just to sit in the back of the temple and smile benevolently, give my good wishes. She said of course and gave me the address of the temple.

I had a plan. I was going to win Mike back. He loved me once; I was certain he could love me again. I would take the train to New Haven, wear a large hat and dark glasses, and sit in the back of the temple until I caught a glimpse of Mike. I would walk quietly over to him, unveil myself. Although he would be surprised, Mike would be thrilled to see me. I would proclaim my stupidity and undying love and then, just like Katharine Ross and Dustin Hoffman in *The Graduate*, Mike and I would go running out of the temple, laughing and breathless, happy to renew our love before it was lost forever.

As I was getting dressed for this reunion, Jace, my college roommate, paid me a surprise visit. Where are you going so dressed up, she asked, and what is that thing you have on your head? I considered lying, but she was my best friend and I decided to enlist her support.

"Mike is getting married today and I'm going to his wedding."

"You're doing what?"

"I'm going to Mike Goldman's wedding. I realize that I've made a terrible mistake and I'm going to get him back. This is my last chance."

"You're not going anywhere, Gene, if I have to tie your hands and legs together. You never loved him, you still don't love him, and the only reason you want him now is that you can't have him. Take off the hat and let's go to the movies."

⊛✖⊛

Jace was wrong about Mike and me. His presence gladdened me, excited me, comforted me. I found him tender and interested, passionate and respectful. My problem wasn't Mike. My problem was that I didn't equate those feelings with love. Love was tense, unpredictable, and urgent. Love was the feeling in my stomach that he was slipping and I had to do something before it was too late. Love was all up to me.

⊛✖⊛

During the first twenty minutes of being with Matt, I knew I wanted to spend my life with him. When I saw Jace the next day, I told her I was madly in love—that I had met the man with whom I was going to spend my life.

"I spoke to you three days ago and you didn't mention anything about love. How long have you known him?" she asked.

"Twenty-four hours," I replied. She rolled her eyes. Jace had seen me through every one of my relationships from the time I was eighteen. She was the only person I told about my relationship with Nick, the married man. That story—and my pain at being with him—came out the weekend I visited her in New Orleans. Over oysters at Casamento's I told her that I had become friendly with a man whom I liked; during our walk in City Park, I told her that he was married; while folding cotton pants in Betty's laundromat, I told her that we had made love once; before we went to sleep the second night, I told her that I spoke to him every day. Finally, she said, "I want the whole truth and I want you to tell it to me now. I won't judge you for any of it. Just tell me what is going on."

About Matt she said, "You've known him twenty-four hours and you're madly in love? That's healthy, Gene, very healthy."

"This one's different," I replied, smiling.

And he was.

My romantic fantasies about meeting The One and getting married in a midnight ceremony with ten thousand candles floating on a lake bloomed again. I will wear the white beaded dress with slits up the side, the one I saw in the window of I. Magnin's over Christmas. I will look smashing, like a shorter, wider Cher. We will write our vows, we will look deep into each other's eyes.

Years of political convictions about the banalities of legal procedures, and about marriage being a heterosexual noose that unfairly excluded my lesbian friends, disappeared like the green flash in the moment after sunset. I wanted to marry Matt. And like every other girl who grew up with Hayley Mills, I wanted Matt to do the asking.

After nine months of writing the guest list in my head and my father's calling and saying, "So?" and my mother's calling and saying, "I promised I wouldn't ask you this, but when are you getting married?" and Matt's mother's calling and saying, "I'm really not an interfering mother-in-law but I have to know: when's the big date?" and my friends saying, "Is it serious?" (meaning "When are you getting married?") and after a particularly loving weekend together, and after waiting as long as I thought humanly fair and after reminding myself that I was a liberated woman and didn't have to wait for the man to do something, I decided to ask Matt myself.

He was sitting across from me in the brown velveteen chair with sunburst designs.

"I have a question to ask you." Heart pounds, stomach turns. "Yes?"

"Will you marry me?" Dumb, I think to myself, at least you could have led into this softly, with a kiss or something.

"We really are so in love, aren't we?"

Is this a trick question? "Yes . . ." I say falteringly, waiting for the bomb to drop.

"And I really do want to marry you . . ." his voice trails through the back door and out into the forest.

I begin to perspire; the sweat is trickling down my sides. I am still waiting.

". . . but I'm not ready to get married."

Love turns to fear, fear hardens to anger, anger becomes embarrassment. I asked him to marry me and he doesn't want to. I wait my whole life to find someone I love enough to marry and now the schmuck doesn't want to marry me. I want to stand up and walk out the door. I don't want to look at him again. His eyes are beady and his hair is like Brillo and his neck is too big.

"I'm just not ready to make a public statement like that. Not this close to Lou Ann's death." He looks at me, notices that every part of me but my body has left the room, and begins to talk very fast. "It has nothing to do with you, Geneenie, it really doesn't. I'm in love with you, I couldn't be happier with anyone, we're so right for each other, it's just something I feel deep inside, it's too soon, I can't do it, it wouldn't be fair to you or to me. When I make that kind of commitment, I want to shout it to the world, I want to be all there, I want to be thrilled about marrying you— and I will be, I just need more time."

Fuck you, fuck Lou Ann, fuck this whole relationship. This is not a polite or empathetic thing to say out loud, so I don't. But I am furious. And injured. I made myself vulnerable, I asked him to marry me, for Godsakes, and he turned me down.

"Talk to me, Geneen."

There's nothing to say.

Five minutes ago I loved him so much I asked him to marry me and now I can't believe I have to sit in the same room with the creep.

"Geneen? Don't make me play guessing games with you. I know you must feel hurt, but tell me what you're thinking. Do you think that I don't love you and that's why I don't want to marry you now?"

I nod my head yes, count to three, and push the words out of my throat. "We've been together for nine months, during which time you've told me that you want to spend the rest of your life with me, you've told me how in love you are with me, but now when I ask you to marry me, to make our commitment public, you tell me you're not ready. I feel like a woman who's been told her husband has been having an affair—all this time I thought you were present and engaged with me and now you say that there's a part of you that hasn't ever been there and still isn't ready to be fully with me."

He answered me, then I sulked and answered him, then he answered me, then I answered him.

Hours later—after tears, a walk in the forest and tamale pie— Matt said: I do love you, I do want to be with you and I am still not fully present. I need to wait three years from the time Lou Ann died before we begin talking about marriage.

I said: I love you too and I hate it that you turned me down and next time it's your turn to ask.

When the three-year anniversary passed, I held my breath each time his eyes misted and he looked as if he was about to say something meaningful. I hoped, I threw the *I Ching*, I wished on the first star. I liked him, I loved him, but my wish was clear: that he would never ask me to marry him.

It was safe to want marriage when he wasn't ready for it. It was familiar to rage about something I couldn't have. It was comforting to be the one pushing against the distance, pulling for greater intimacy. I knew how to act healthy; I knew how to pretend to be vulnerable; I knew how to look like an adult. But I didn't know how to be any of those. And until I met Matt, I didn't know that I didn't know.

The hard part wasn't meeting Matt. The hard part is staying with him. The hard part is staying anywhere. When I knew Matt for six months, I wrote in my journal, "If I'm always leaving, I can't be left. I *will not* be the steady one, the regular, the chump, waiting at the dinner table for the man who never comes home, making myself available to be made a fool of. When I'm still and quiet, I'm a target. When I'm moving, no one can catch me, hit me, hurt me."

❃✖❃

In eighth grade, my friend Sharon told me about a boy she met named Larry Klein. They dated for two months, but she broke up with him because he was bossy and mean and had a hooked nose. Later that year, I transferred to another school and met Larry. Sharon had broken his heart, but he had mended it and was now going steady with Laura Boxer. I wanted Larry. When he got mononucleosis, I visited him every day. I climbed into bed with him and kissed him, let him put his hands up my blouse. By the time he was better, he had broken up with Laura, given me his ID bracelet, and was asking me to go to the World's Fair with him on weekends. I tolerated him for three months, then I decided he was mean and bossy and had a hooked nose.

I always got involved with men who didn't want me or couldn't be with me. And the relationship always looked as if I was ready to commit myself and was being frustrated by lovers who couldn't find their feelings. As long as he was the asshole, I could afford to have love flowing through my veins. I could flutter and fuss and wait, all the while knowing that it was hopeless and that the distance between us would be maintained. If a man happened to be available, I could rely on my obsession with food to keep me from being intimate because it kept me from myself.

The distance was comforting. During the two years that Ralph, the meditator, was traveling around the world, I was sitting in my blue-and-green apartment listening to the theme song from *Tootsie* and crooning to the image of Ralph's face and the illusion of love.

As long as it was only the potential of a relationship that I was in love with—the images, the illusion—I didn't have to be vulnerable. Like putting my life on hold until I got thin. Nothing counted until I got thin because once I got thin, everything would change. I was living on top of myself, waiting for my life to get real.

I back-doored myself with Matt. I got involved with a man who was involved with another woman. A dead woman was enough of a woman to create comfortable distance. Something stood between us, something that kept him from being fully present, something to rage against. Something to pull for and strive for and wish for. Without Matt's grief about Lou Ann, there was nothing between us but what each of us chose to put there. It wasn't the illusion of intimacy any more; it was the real thing. And I was terrified.

A woman came to me after she lost sixty pounds on a diet and gained seventy pounds back. She was furious that being thin wasn't what it was cracked up to be. Without the Dream-of-Being-Thin happiness when she was fat, she had nothing standing between her and being fully alive. And she didn't like it.

You can't stay thin if you are not ready to give up the illusion and face yourself. And you can't stay in a relationship, a healthy, growing one, if you are not willing to stop focusing on what's wrong with the other person and be truthful with yourself. Breaking free from compulsive eating and participating in a mutually supportive relationship require the same thing: the willingness to stop defending yourself against pain.

Being in a relationship is painful. But it's real pain. It's not the pain of wanting someone who doesn't want you, nor is it the pain of trying to fix someone's life so that they see the truth— or you. Breaking free from compulsive eating is painful as well, but it's not the pain of getting on a scale and seeing that you've gained four pounds or of eating something you shouldn't have or of wanting to be thin when you are fat. Real pain happens when you take away what's standing between you and being awake. It's the gritty pain of growing yourself up. It's the dark and dirty pain of acknowledging that you are forty years old and still afraid of telling your father the truth. Real pain is pain with hair on it, animal pain that comes from the cave in you. It's the pain of shaking off what you've taken on and isn't yours so that you can step into the shimmer of a life that is yours.

The pain of a compulsion is not real pain. Neither is the pain of being with an unavailable or abusive partner. I don't mean to say that you don't hurt, only that the hurt is piled on top of the deeper, truer, hurt. There is original pain, pain of loss, loneliness, sorrow, fear. And there is the pain you create to distract yourself from feeling loss, loneliness, sorrow, fear. There is pain and there is pain on top of pain. Healing is about opening the wound and letting it heal from the inside out, exposing it to wind and sun and time, not piling bandages on it and screaming each time your skin gets caught in the adhesive tape.

The nature of obsession is that it protects you from the truth. Relationships are a process of facing, then stripping away, the layers you have constructed between you and allowing someone to make a difference to you.

I remember the day I realized that although I was living my life around food, what I could eat and couldn't eat, and although I would die for a hot fudge sundae and although nothing, and I mean nothing, was as good as food, I didn't *like* food. I didn't look at it, didn't smell it, didn't taste it, didn't notice its subtleties. Food was incidental to the purpose for which I used it. I happened to be eating, but what I really wanted was to stop the ruckus inside.

I used food and I used people. I called the food part compulsive eating and I called the people part love. I used both of them for the same purpose: to avoid feeling my fear, my shame about being myself, my hopelessness about being alive. I didn't pay much attention to the kinds of food I ate or the people I chose. I chose chocolate less for its taste (after the first bite, I stopped tasting) than for how I felt when I was finished eating it. I chose lovers less for what they could offer me than for how much fixing our relationships demanded. My goal in eating and loving was exactly the same: I wanted to be taken away from myself.

❧✖☙

There were many moments as a compulsive eater when I was afraid that if I didn't eat it all today, now, this second, it would be gone when I next wanted it. It wasn't that this piece of cake or lasagne would be gone but that I was giving up an opportunity, maybe my last, to fill the part of me that was forever hungry, forever desperate for relief. I could never honestly say that I had enough, because although my body was full, I was empty. And I was convinced that somewhere in the next bite or piece or slice was enough.

I taught myself to stop eating compulsively. I put food in plastic bags, a cookie in one bag, a piece of cheese in another. I carried the bags with me. I traveled with dried pears and rice crackers, baked tofu sandwiches and red licorice, and told myself over and over that anytime I was hungry I could eat, I didn't have to eat it all now. It worked. The constant reassurance that I wasn't losing anything by not eating the whole thing at this moment allowed me to feel safe. I learned to eat when I was hungry and stop when my body had enough. I lost weight. Food is not a problem any more. But the hunger remained.

When Matt was about to leave on a trip, he became my last

chance, my hope of finding relief. In that moment, the urgency did not seem as though it was about anything but wanting him to stay—just as, in eating, the urgency didn't seem as though it was about anything but wanting to binge. Matt became my food: the desire for one final burst of bittersweet chocolate, the last gasp of ice cream, my only chance to be whole. In the moment before he walked out the door, I was desperate for him to fill something I didn't know was missing until it was apparent that he would no longer be available to fill it. I wanted all of him—now—and could not put him in plastic bags for later.

The essence of compulsion is the belief that the power to fill ourselves, to make ourselves whole, rests outside of us. If we feel that something or someone can right what is wrong, then we will become compulsive about having it always.

Compulsion is not necessarily about a substance or an activity. We are compulsive because of the way we feel about ourselves. There is a quality to the way we live our lives that is either compulsive or not compulsive. It is not about food or drink or drugs or work, although we may engage in those things compulsively. The hallmark of a compulsion is the inability to know when we've had enough. Of anything. Food, work, love, success, money.

The hardest part about compulsion is that when the behavior ends, the emptiness does not.

I thought, I really believed, I was absolutely counting on, a relationship to make me happy. I didn't know that being in a mutually supportive, loving, and respectful relationship was my last holdout and that once I met Matt and had no big dream to wish for, I would come face to face with the fragmented and split-off parts of myself that I hadn't dared to acknowledge.

❂✖❂

Suzuki Roshi, a Zen master, said that "nothing happens outside of you." A relationship is not about finding peace by being with another human being. It is about making a commitment to maintain contact and not run away when your partner is a mirror for the hardness in your heart.

Matt cannot heal me. But if I am willing not to run away, not to eat compulsively, not to find another lover, not to retreat into my work, I will find the face beneath my face. And I will heal myself.

The question is not when or if you will meet someone you love; nothing will change when you meet the love of your life except that you will have met the love of your life. The work begins when the infatuation ends. And the question is not how glorious it will be to wake up with a warm body beside you and have someone to go to the movies with and celebrate holidays with and go to your parents' house with and be yourself with. The question is what will you do when it gets hard. How can you trust someone when you've never learned to trust yourself? What does it mean for someone who has replaced love with food to be in a loving relationship? What do we need to learn about intimacy? What does being intimate with one person teach us about our connection to all living things?

❀✖❀

If you deeply explore one area of life, you will find the answers to every area. What you learn as you break free from your obsession with food is what you need to learn about intimacy:

> Commit yourself.
> Tell the truth.
> Trust yourself.
> Pain ends and so does everything else.
> Laugh easily.
> Cry easily.
> Have patience.

Be willing to be vulnerable.
When you notice that you are clinging to anything and it's
   causing trouble, drop it.
Be willing to fail.
Don't let fear stop you from leaping into the unknown or
   from sitting in dark silence.
Remember that everything gets lost, stolen, ruined, worn
   out, or broken; bodies sag and wrinkle; everyone suf-
   fers; and everyone dies.
No act of love is ever wasted.

ലൂX

People come into a workshop wanting a miracle. They want to
be thin yesterday. They are tired of dealing with their obsession
with food, tired from having spent a good deal of their lives
thinking about their bodies, what they can eat, what they can't
eat, what they just ate that they shouldn't have eaten. They want
it to be over. They want to get on with their lives. I tell them
give yourself a year of following the Breaking Free program and
they look at me as if I've lost my mind. Then the people who
have been following the eating guidelines for a year stand up and
talk about what it feels like to eat when they are hungry and not
use food to replace love, comfort, self-expression. The new people
want to know how. How did you have the courage to stick with
this? What makes you different from the other people who tried
and gained weight and felt discouraged and went on a liquid diet
instead?

They made a commitment to the process and they kept it.
They had a vision of what was possible and they followed it.
When they were frightened, they didn't allow the fear to stop
them. They believed in their essential goodness.

Last night I had a dream about a man who was living in
Antarctica, studying the Native Americans there. He had a long

beautiful beard and brown eyes. He asked me where Cupertino was and if he could get there by walking. His house was made of bird's eye maple, and tools were hung everywhere on the walls. Even though I was living with Matt, I considered moving in with him, he was so sexy. It would be a rough life, I thought to myself—outhouses, no hot water. Reinventing the wheel one more time. Then I woke up.

I have a friend who put off getting married until he was forty-three because he was waiting to meet Natassja Kinski and marry her. He lived in Berkeley, was a computer programmer, didn't travel. Last night, I dreamed about moving in with a mountain man. As much as I love Matt, there is a part of me that doesn't want to admit that this is it, I'm not going anywhere. I can't run away with Harry Hamlin and discover bliss.

When people come to workshops, they keep the option of dieting in their back pockets. Well, okay, we'll try this for a week, a month, but if it doesn't work or if we get too scared, if we gain weight or if friends make fun of us, there's always a diet.

For the first four days of a meditation retreat, I think about all the ways I am going to leave. Borrow someone's car, take a bus, call a friend, rent a helicopter. Then I realize that the only thing worse than staying is leaving. I can't get away from myself.

In my previous books I spoke of treating ourselves with kindness and gentleness and compassion. I still believe that all three of those are necessary parts of breaking free. But there is one ingredient that I didn't mention and it is the glue that holds the other parts together: effort and commitment. Not leaving when it gets hard.

We wouldn't be compulsive eaters if we knew how to stay when it got hard. But we have to practice. We have to pretend we know how to live. Making a commitment to a way of eating or to a relationship is the same: the commitment is to a way of living in the world. The commitment is to staying with yourself, not another person, not an eating program—and arranging your eating, work, relationships, and spiritual life according to your priorities. Doing what you need to do to let the life within you unfold and not letting yourself be seduced by glamour, money, fame, thinness, or the illusion that you can live a life free of pain.

❀✖❀

Counting backward from Matt over the last twenty years, I've been with a man who was not attracted to me, a man I didn't like, a married man, a married woman, a man who lived in London, a man of whom I was frightened, a man who lived in Buffalo, a man for whom I felt no passion, a man who died.

If it wasn't frantic or tumultuous, it wasn't love. To love, you had to long for. To love, you had to bleed.

After almost three years of being with him, I told Sara that I couldn't decide whether Matt was one of the most superficial, repressed human beings on earth or one of the most patient and compassionate men alive.

My relationship with Matt is easy. By "easy," I mean that I don't have to burn my fingernails, take charge of his mental health or his relationship with his mother, cook more than butternut squash and artichokes, be neater than he is, act like Melanie in *Gone With the Wind*, use sex to convince him to love me, or pretend that I am anyone less than the complex, principled, outspoken, and mercurial being that I am.

He loves me when I carry crackers, biscotti, dried fruit, and amazake rice milk on airplanes in addition to a carry-on bag, luggage wheels, brightly colored shopping bags. He loves me when I wake up frightened in the middle of the night and ask him to sing to me. He loves me when I take three days to make a decision and three more days to change the decision I made.

He loves me when I insist we make tofu dogs over the mesquite grill in the backyard and it takes two hours to make the fire and two minutes to throw the shriveled tofu on top of the lemon rinds in the compost pile.

He does not: hit me, change radically from one day or moment to the next day or moment, expect me to take care of him, pull on me—either directly or indirectly—to stop taking care of myself, need me to feel comfortable about himself or his life. He does not collapse when I act like a three-year-old and believe that the only way I can get what I want is if he caves in.

He does: see what's luminous about me and encourage it, see what's troubled about me and accept it, pursue his dreams with passion and regardless of my approval, wake up grinning, laugh with me and cry before me, confront me when I am unfair, remind me who I am when I have forgotten why I am alive. He tells the truth.

❧✖❧

Being loved by and loving one person teaches you what is possible with other people, with all living things. Being intimate or being distant, telling the truth or hiding from it, are decisions you make on a daily basis, countless times, in countless situations—at the grocery store, at the gas station, when someone cuts you off on the freeway, when you pass by a homeless person, when you hear that two-hundred-year-old trees are being destroyed and that your grandchildren may never see a virgin forest.

It matters whether you see yourself as someone who is capable of effecting change or whether you see yourself as someone whose voice does not count. It matters whether you treat yourself with reverence or with carelessness. Every bit of work you do on yourself matters. Every time you choose love, it matters.

When food is love, love is hard and lacquer-shiny. Love is outside of you, another thing to acquire and make yours. When love is love, there is nothing standing between you and your breaking heart.

Love moves you. And that is good.

Available from
GENEEN ROTH

ISBN 978-0-452-26254-6   ISBN 978-0-452-26818-0   ISBN 978-0-452-27083-1

ISBN 978-0-452-27679-6   ISBN 978-0-452-28491-3

www.geneenroth.com

Available wherever books are sold.